First Nibbles of the Apple Computer

Publishing Director: David Culverwell
Acquisitions Editor: Susan Love
Production Editor: Roberta Glencer
Art Director/Cover Design: Don Sellers
Assistant Art Director: Bernard Vervin
Manufacturing Director: John A. Komsa

Typesetter: Electronic Publishing Services, Baltimore, MD
Printer: Semline, Inc., Westwood, MA
Typefaces: Century Schoolbook (text), Univers (display)

First Nibbles of the Apple Computer

A "You Can Do It" Beginners' Manual written in Applesoft BASIC
for the Apple II, Apple II Plus, Apple IIe, and Apple IIc

Melba Bennett

Brady Communications Company, Inc.
A Prentice-Hall Publishing Company
Bowie, Maryland 20715

First Nibbles of the Apple Computer

Library of Congress Cataloging in Publication Data

Bennett, Melba, 1930—
First "Nibbles" of the Apple computer.

Includes index.

Summary: A beginner's introduction to the Apple computer explaining the basic aspects of word processing, programming, and application with simple instructions, illustrations, and examples.

1. Apple II (Computer)—Programming—Juvenile literature. 2. Apple IIe (Computer)—Programming—Juvenile literature. 3. Apple II Plus (Computer)—Programming—Juvenile literature. 4. Basic (Computer program language)—Juvenile literature. [1. Apple IIe (Computer)—Programming. 2. Apple II Plus (Computer)—Programming. 3. Basic (Computer program language) 4. Programming (Computers) 5. Programming languages (Computers)] I. Title.
QA76.8.A662B46 1984 001.64'2 84-11183
ISBN 0-89303-456-8

Prentice-Hall International, Inc., *London*
Prentice-Hall Canada, Inc.,, Scarborough, *Ontario*
Prentice-Hall of Australia, Pty., Ltd., *Sydney*
Prentice-Hall of India Private Limited, *New Delhi*
Prentice-Hall of Japan, Inc.,, *Tokyo*
Prentice-Hall of Southeast Asia Pte. Ltd., *Singapore*
Whitehall Books, Limited, Petone, *New Zealand*
Editora Prentice-Hall Do Brasil LTDA., *Rio de Janeiro*
Prentice-Hall Hispanoamericana, S.A., *Mexico*

Printed in the United States of America

85 86 87 88 89 90 91 92 93 94 95 1 2 3 4 5 6 7 8 9 10

Dedication

I dedicate this book to my best friend, my companion, my sweetheart, my handyman, my artist, my "punny man," my confidant, my guitarist, my playmate—all the same person—my husband, Stan.

And I also dedicate it to you, as a modern "pioneer" forging ahead, trying to learn about computers. It will make a better world for all of us if you put your new computer knowledge to work serving and teaching others.

Contents

Preface

This book was written with an emphasis on the human element of using a computer. Computer technology is changing at a "head-spinning" pace! People need to develop greater self-confidence, self-mastery, and flexibility to overcome computer anxiety.

This book can help you gain more confidence and self-knowledge as you learn how to control a computer. Many comparisons are made to the known situations of life that are similar, in theory, to the workings of a computer. You will go from the known to the unknown in a step-by-step fashion; you will be encouraged to keep trying, even when learning about computers may become challenging and somewhat frustrating.

A basic understanding of how a computer functions, the ability to use software programs, and the development of skills in communicating and getting along with others are becoming essential. This book will teach you how to use the Apple II, Apple II Plus, Apple IIe, or Apple IIc computer and possibly develop a healthier attitude in the process!

It's always easier to learn when you can have a laugh or two to relieve tenson. The old "spoonful of sugar helping the medicine go down" works! Tongue-in-cheek humor, supplied by Nibbles, the electronic worm, is sprinkled throughout the book, along with thoughts to encourage and motivate.

Many people have helped with this book. Our entire family has worked working with it. Treat the computer as you would a new co-worker who needs to be told everything to do but who will work harder than anyone when orders are clear and understandable. Our family, the "Bennett Bunch," calls our computer Nibbles. This makes us feel more like our computer, Nibbles, is a member of the family, making it easier to work out problems "together."

Many people have helped with this book. Our entire family has worked together on this project. Lisa did lots of extra chores to give Mom more time to work at the computer. Dean has given much good advice about various programs and did all the drawings for the first manuscript, which was used at Deer Valley High School for two years. Stan has given much-needed moral support, as well as many hours at the drawing board creating roughs for the cartoons, writing captions, and editing.

Stan, Dean, and Lisa all have shown much love and patience and have encouraged the development of Nibbles and his message!

We hope you and your family grow closer together, as we have, by sharing this book and the adventure of learning something as stimulating and challenging as programming! Old fashion love for one another and faith in ourselves and our maker will help us all as we look forward to a great tomorrow!

The future belongs to those who are prepared for it!

Many people have helped make this book a reality. I wish to express my gratitude to Sue Love, Acquisitions Editor at Brady Communications Company, for her warmth, enthusiasm, and belief in *Nibbles*. Sue's last name

describes the service she gives to others. I appreciate my reviewers' time, interest, and effort. Their suggestions and comments have helped a great deal. Bobbie Glencer, Production Editor, also deserves recognition for her work and interest in this book.

Dr. Gary Bitter, of Arizona State University, guided me as I wrote the first edition of *Nibbles*, which was used at Deer Valley High School for two years. Dr. Bitter's inspiration helped make publishing this enlarged, revised edition possible.

I am also grateful to the Deer Valley Unified School District—Dr. Keith McSpadden and Sandy Abram in particular—for their support. The principal of Deer Valley High, Robert Sauter, and Business Dept. Chairman, Richard Russell, also have been supportive and helpful.

My friends at The Computer Store in Phoenix—Dana Krieger and Bob McMaster—have furnished expert advice and helped solve some technical problems, for which I am grateful. They give the type of service that makes owning a computer a nice experience.

I gratefully acknowledge Apple Computer, Inc., for letting us reproduce certain information, sketches, illustration, and pictures from their various publications. A special thanks goes to Sue Espinoza of Apple for her excellent suggestions.

Now let me introduce you to Nibbles!

Nibbles is an electronic worm who likes to help people learn to use the Apple computer. He will be your guide as you read this book.

Look for him. . .he'll be found on many pages to help you have a laugh or two as you learn about computers!

He has a good sense of humor. . .for an electronic worm!

Limits of Liability and Disclaimer of Warranty

Trademarks of Material Mentioned in This Text

Note to Authors

Have you written a book related to personal computers? Do you have an idea for developing such a project? If so, we would like to hear from you. Brady produces a complete range of books for the personal computer market. We invite you to write to David Culverwell, Publishing Director, Brady Communications Company, Inc., Bowie, MD 20715.

About the Author

Melba Bennett has spent over 25 years teaching business education, public relations, self improvement, private voice, and music classes in high schools and colleges. She currently teaches introductory computer courses, BASIC programming, and keyboarding at Deer Valley High School in Glendale, Arizona, a suburb of Phoenix, Arizona. Her degrees include an Associate of Arts, a Bachelor of Fine Arts, and a Master of Science. She is listed in Who's Who of American Women.

Born in Salt Lake City, Utah, Melba moved to Phoenix after receiving her degrees from the University of Utah. While teaching in Phoenix, she met her husband, Stan. They now have two children, one dog, one cockateel bird and two Apple computers.

Melba, a mezzo-soprano, has appeared professionally in operas, musical comedies, concerts, and recitals in the United States and Canada and has trained many singers and speakers to more effectively use their voices. She believes that developing a positive mental attitude is essential to master any challenging skill—whether it is learning to sing or to use a computer.

1
INTRODUCTION

Welcome to the computer generation!

Congratulations on deciding to learn about computers! The more you and your family understand how a computer works, the more at home you will feel in this computer generation. Our entire society is being affected by computers; the changes brought about by computers are as great as the changes brought about by the invention of the wheel. With the coming of the wheel, mankind began to travel greater distances. Now with computers, mankind can travel vast mental distances using computer circuitry "wheels of knowledge." Computers have unlocked great sources of knowledge, and this is only the beginnning.

The computer can do many jobs for you.

The computer takes much of the drudgery out of work. Arithmetic is calculated on a computer with great accuracy and speed; hundreds of letters and reports can be processed and printed with very little effort. The patient computer can be used for teaching almost any subject and, of course, can be used for entertainment. Anyone for a computer game?

Computers and television both need programs.

Your television set is not useful without a television program, and your computer isn't useful without its programs. Both pieces of equipment must be programmed in order to operate. There are many kinds of computer programs with various purposes or applications, just as there are many kinds of television programs.

Excellent programs are available for you to use.

It won't be necessary for you to write all your own programs. Even top T.V. personalities don't write all of their own material. There is a great variety of programs written by professional programmers for many different applications to be used on Apple II, Apple II Plus, Apple IIe, and Apple IIc computers. One of the

many outstanding features of the Apple computer is the great abundance of software that is available.

Computer programs are often called software.

Computers are similar to a human mind.

A computer is designed to resemble a human mind. The human mind is the most magnificent computer ever made! Man-made computers are really quite unimpressive when compared to the mind and what it can accomplish.

Information first comes into the mind through the eyes, ears, and other senses. This is called input. This information goes into the memory and is stored for later use.

When you think about what you see, hear, touch, taste, or smell, you are processing the information. After you have received your input and processed the information, you can now produce output. Speaking and writing are two forms of output. For example, when you are introduced to someone new, you see a face and hear a name. Your mind processes and stores in memory the person's facial image, plus the name you heard as you were introduced.

Your mind does this type of action millions of times a day. Can you think of some other examples?

YOUR MIND DOES THIS TYPE OF ACTION MILLIONS OF TIMES A DAY.
CAN YOU THINK OF SOME OTHERS?

Develop a good attitude.

Most everyone agrees it is helpful to have a good attitude. Here are several suggestions to help you develop a good attitude, which will help make learning about computers more enjoyable.

1. Begin each new chapter with enthusiasm and calmness.
2. Be patient. Don't expect to know everything immediately.
3. Congratulate yourself as you progress and learn some new material. Say "Hurray for me!"
4. Give your computer a name, such as Nibbles, to help make your relationship with your computer more fun.
5. Believe in your ability to learn to operate a computer.

6. Realize it is not necessary to be a genius to learn to use a computer. Anyone who spends sufficient time and effort can learn to operate the Apple or any other computer.
7. Develop a strong desire to learn about computers.
8. Find someone to answer your questions when you need help or advice in operating a computer.
8. Make a commitment to keep going. Never give up when things seem too difficult. You build self-mastery and self-control when you stick to something you have started.
9. Smile, not frown, as you learn. Learning comes easier when you are trying to enjoy it. Relax tense muscles in the back of your neck as you sit at the computer. Develop the habit of taking deep breaths to give you "relaxed energy."
10. Believe you can do it! It can be done!

A GOOD ATTITUDE HELPS YOU LEARN.

Keep your life in balance.

It is very important to keep your life in balance while you are studying computers. Be certain to get proper rest, exercise, diet, and social life; keep up in any other subjects you are studying. Don't study computers and nothing else! You will need to know

a great deal about English, math, and many subjects if you are going to use your computer knowledge to the best advantage in your life. You need to know many things if you want to be a professional computer programmer or hope to have some high-level computer position.

Some people have made themselves ill by overdoing the time and interest they spend with computers. Eye strain, sore back and neck muscles, fatigue and many other problems have developed from improper use of the computer. Keep everything in moderation . . . even using the computer!

Learn to get along with others.

Communications and public relations skills are becoming more essential. Learning to express yourself clearly as you speak and write will help to make your computer skills even more valuable.

The more you can be of service to help solve problems for others, the more successful and happy you will be. Learn to deal with other human beings, not just your computer. People—not things—bring happiness. Work on your relationships with other people.

The more well-balanced and happy you are, the more creative you can become in using the computer.

LEARN TO COMMUNICATE WITH OTHER PEOPLE!

Learn to solve problems and set goals.

Problem-solving ability is very necessary in learning how to use a computer. You must know what you wish to accomplish before you can begin. It's like knowing your destination before you start out on a trip. You can waste a lot of gas and time if you haven't decided on your destination and start going in the wrong direction.

BE A PROBLEM SOLVER!

Goal-setting in life is even more necessary. You are much more likely to accomplish what you wish to do if you have a definite purpose for doing something—especially something that is going to take time and effort.

List the reasons why you wish to learn how to use a computer—to let your mind know that learning computers is really important to you. This will give you a definite purpose and your mind will be "programmed" to help you reach your goal.

What your mind can believe, you will be able to achieve, if you are willing to give the proper time and effort.

HOW CAN I REACH MY GOAL?

LIST YOUR GOALS AND THE METHODS YOU WILL USE TO ACCOMPLISH THEM

These are some reasons I want to learn to use a computer:

1.

2.

3.

4.

5.

This is my goal:

I will accomplish my goal by doing the following:

1.

2.

3.

4.

When you know what you want to do in life, you automatically start doing things that help you accomplish your goal!

Become acquainted with this book.

In order to get the most benefit from any book, you should know how to use it properly and know how it is organized.

This beginner's manual was designed to help you by having a nice guide—Nibbles—lead you from one lesson to the next. You will find his picture throughout the book to let you know you are not alone. He is going to be with you all the way.

By giving clear instructions, illustrations and examples, and lots of encouragement, Nibbles hopes to make this one of the greatest learning adventures you've ever had!

GET ACQUAINTED WITH THIS BOOK!

There is an inspirational thought at the start of each lesson. Each lesson has a stated goal so you'll know what you are trying to accomplish. Knowing these goals should help your mind get prepared to receive new data or information.

Most lessons in this book are arranged in a similar manner.

Each chapter begins with a listing of new words that are found in that chapter. Next comes the new information written in paragraph style. There will be program examples for you to study to help gain greater understanding of the new ideas.

Then it will be your turn to be creative and do some original writing using concepts you've learned. Self-quizzes are at the end of each chapter so you can make certain you've really learned the lesson. No one has to see your test score. It will be our secret if you want to go back and reread the chapter to get a better understanding of the lesson.

A list of the new vocabulary and definitions will be at the conclusion of most chapters.

Does that give you an idea of how it will be? Good. Let's get started. On with the learning!

WOW! SUCH EAGER LEARNERS!

2
COMPUTER HARDWARE

GOAL: To become acquainted with Apple II, Apple II Plus, Apple IIe, and Apple IIc hardware.

THOUGHT: Anything you keep doing becomes more enjoyable and easier.

Aa Bb Cc Dd Ee Ff Gg Hh Ii Jj Kk Ll Mm

Vocabulary To Learn:

COMPUTER	KEYBOARD	PRINTER
HARDWARE	DISK DRIVE	INPUT
MONITOR	DISK	OUTPUT
PROCESSOR	AUXILIARY STORAGE	MEMORY

Whenever you begin to learn a new subject, you should make friends with the words frequently used. Try to become acquainted with the terms listed on the blackboard.

Don't try to learn all these new words at once. Just be on the lookout when you see them in this chapter and try to remember what they mean.

IT'S IMPORTANT TO LEARN AND UNDERSTAND COMPUTER VOCABULARY.

Which kind of Apple computer are you using?

Just as apples you eat come in various flavors, the Apple computer comes in assorted models.

Check the front of your computer to see which kind of Apple you are using and fill out the next line.

I am using an ____________________(type of Apple computer.)

This beginners' manual was designed to be used with the Apple IIe, Apple IIc, Apple II, or Apple II Plus.

The booklet which came with your computer when you bought it will be helpful in giving you specific instructions about your particular machine.

DO YOU HAVE AN APPLE II? AN APPLE IIe?

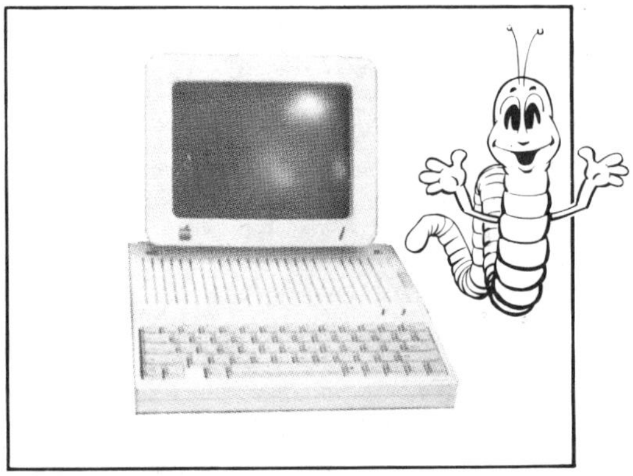

OR AN APPLE IIc?

The various parts of computer equipment are called **hardware**. Hardware usually consists of a **monitor**, a computer **processor** with its **keyboard**, a **disk drive** or **drives** and a **printer**.

Information comes in as **input** through the keyboard or disk drive. Then the information goes into the processor where it is rearranged and made more useful. Next the data is sent to the monitor or printer as **output**.

The computer monitor is similar to a TV screen.

The **monitor** looks like an old friend of yours—the TV. In fact, you can use a TV as a monitor if a special adaptor is added to the TV. However, computer monitors are preferred, because they are easier to read than a TV screen.

Before turning on the computer, check the monitor to see if it is ready to go. Is the main power cord of the monitor plugged into an alternating current outlet?

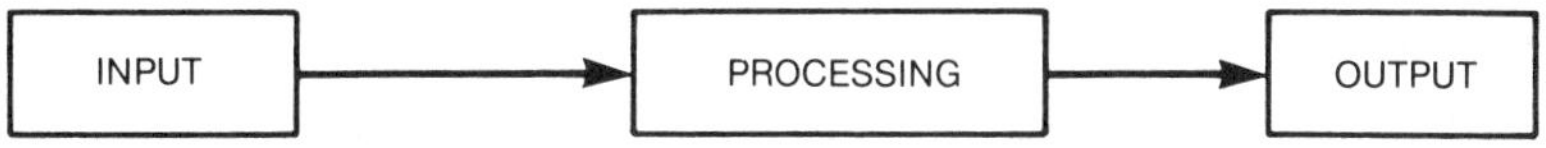

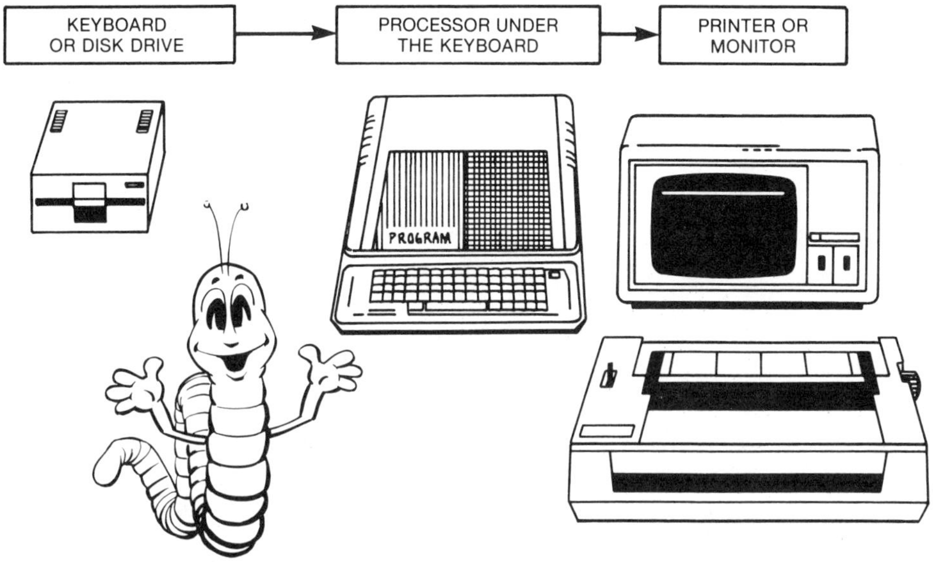

Also check to see if another small cord called the connector jack is plugged firmly into both the video outlet in the back of the computer and the monitor itself. It's a good idea to handle this cord and its connectors carefully to avoid loose connections.

THE MONITOR LOOKS LIKE A TV.

Get ready to turn on the monitor.

The on/off switch for the monitor is located on either the front, top, or right side. The contrast knob is usually found close to the on/off switch. Do you see it?

Fine tuning knobs to adjust "flop over" are usually on the back of the monitor. Can you find these controls?

You'll soon be using the monitor, so get acquainted with it.

The on/off switch is found at the ________________ of my monitor.

The contrast knob is found at the ________________ of my monitor.

The fine tuning knobs are at the ________________ of my monitor.

THE MONITOR IS EASY TO TURN ON AND OFF FOR HUMANS...
BUT IT IS DIFFICULT FOR ELECTRONIC WORMS!

Every computer must have a processor.

The computer contains the **processor**, **memory**, and other electronic circuitry. The processor is a vital part of the computer. Without the processor a computer can't do its "tricks." The processor circuitry is called a chip; the chip used in the Apple II, II Plus and Apple IIe is called the 6502 Chip. The number refers to the design of the chip. Most of the same instructions can be used on all three of these Apple models, partly because they all contain the same type of processor chip. The chip used on the Apple IIc has been modified and is called the 65C02. The Apple IIc has been designed so that most of the programs for the other Apple models can be used on this newer one. New technology is constantly upgrading the quality and performance of computers. The Apple IIc is an example of improvements being made. Computers are becoming more powerful, less expensive, easier to operate, more efficient, smaller and more portable. Older computers can be upgraded with new chips and circuitry; it is well worth the money.

The computer is an electronic machine, so it must be plugged in to operate. One end of the large power supply cord is plugged into the back of the computer and the other end is plugged into an alternating current outlet.

The on/off switch is rather fragile; avoid turning the computer on and off in rapid succession to avoid having to replace this toggle-type switch.

Turn on your computer.

Find the on/off switch for your computer. The switch on the Apple IIc has the on position marked with a Number 1 (1) and the off position with a Zero (0).

The keyboard is part of the computer.

The **keyboard** of the computer is similar to a typewriter keyboard. Again . . . you've found a familiar friend!

THE KEYBOARD LOOKS LIKE A TYPEWRITER.

Disk drives store information on disks.

The **disk drive** is called an **auxiliary storage device.** Information, or data, may be stored on **disks** which look like small phonograph records. When these disks are placed in the disk drive, the information from the disks can be sent to the computer RAM memory and stored until it is processed. Being able to store information outside the computer is very valuable. It's like having extra drawers to store clothes you don't use every day.

Find the disk drive door and lift it to the open position. Now push it down to the closed position. It's a good idea to leave the door closed when the computer is not being used, to keep out dust and dirt which could damage the delicate mechanical parts of the disk drive. The disk drive is both mechanical and electronic. Handle it carefully, according to instructions, to keep it functioning properly.

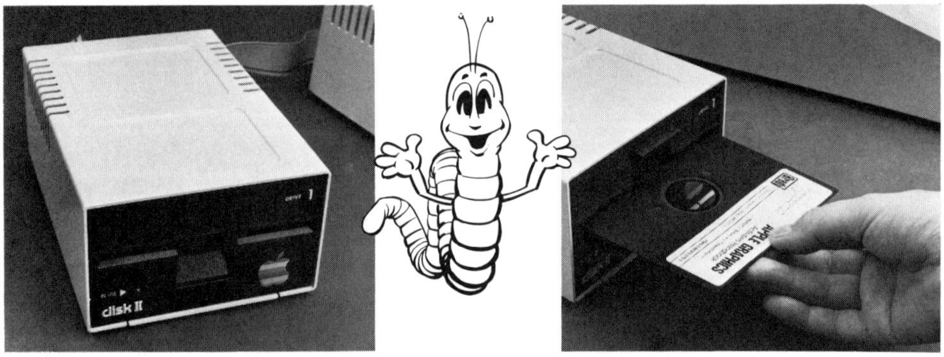

HANDLE DISK DRIVES CAREFULLY!

The disk drive on the Apple IIc is located inside the computer on the right side. To open the door, press inward near the top of the latch. Don't try to push up from the bottom of the door. The latch should pop open easily to allow a disk to be loaded. No forcing is necessary. To close the door, simply press down on the latch. It may feel awkward at first; however, after you experiment and get used to pressing inward, you should have no problems.

Cassette tapes may be used for auxiliary storage.

Cassette tape recorders may be used in place of the disk drive for extra storage on the Apple II, Apple II Plus, and Apple IIe. Cassettes that are used for music or other purposes may be used with the computer. However, tapes used with the cassette tape recorder must be programmed with electronic signals. This can be done from the keyboard and is called key to tape. Touching a key on the keyboard sends a message through the computer memory and processor unit. The message then goes as output to the tape.

The outlet for the cassette is located at the back of the computer on the right side. Read the manual that came with your computer for more information regarding the use of cassettes. The tapes may be used as both input and output—just as disks can be used.

The disk drive and disks are preferable because they are much faster. Cassettes cannot be used with the Apple IIc. Very few people want to use cassettes after they know the advantages of disk storage.

CASSETTES AND TAPES MAY BE USED INSTEAD OF DISK DRIVES.

Printers produce hard copy output.

The **printer** is an **output** device which produces hard copy. Hard copy is material printed on paper you can handle. For example, a letter or card would be considered hard copy. Output on the monitor can only be observed, not handled, so it is not hard copy.

Printers are classified according to speed and quality of printing. Even the slowest printer can print much faster than a person can type on a typewriter. Some printers are "bi-directional," which means they can print in both directions—first with one line printing from left to right; the next, from right to left.

Some printers produce dot matrix printing. From close up, you can see tiny dots which make up the letters. Letter-quality printers produce a higher grade of printing without the dots.

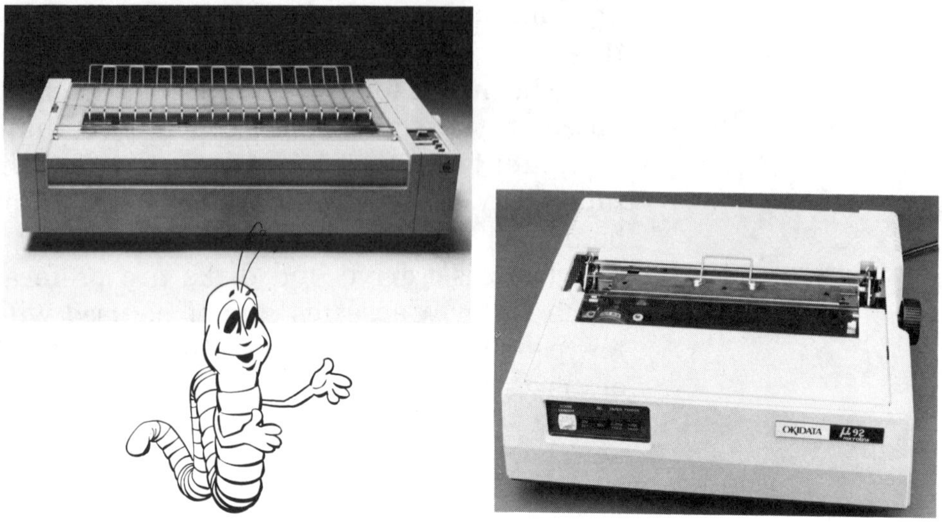

THERE ARE MANY TYPES OF PRINTERS.

Computers use special languages.

All computers must be told what to do in a language they can understand. The BASIC language is commonly used for microcomputers, such as the Apple. But there are many forms or "dialects" of BASIC, just as there are many dialects of English. Applesoft is a BASIC dialect used by the Apple II, Apple II Plus, Apple IIe, and Apple IIc.

Other brands of computers have their own distinctive languages; programs used on an Apple probably will not work on

LEARN TO "SPEAK" A COMPUTER LANGUAGE.

another kind of computer, such as a TRS-80 or IBM PC, unless there are changes made in the program.

This is similar to translating English into another language when you travel to a foreign country. Ideas may be the same, but thoughts have to be reworded to communicate with someone who speaks another language.

Information is stored in RAM and ROM memory.

The **memory** is a vital part of the computer. Visualize rows of small box-like partitions with names or numbers on them, such as those used in offices to store mail for various employees. Mailbox partitions and computer memory are similar; both are numbered and store data.

RAM is one of the two types of memory in the computer. RAM stands for Random Access Memory; you have random access to any memory box without having to first sort through all the other boxes. Another name which is used for RAM and better describes this type of memory is Read and Write Memory, because you can write data into this memory. This is the memory you will use to write your programs. Because data stored in RAM is erased when the computer is turned off, it is always wise to save your work on a disk so you can have a copy of your hard work. Keep a disk in the disk drive.

ROM is the other type of memory. It is called Read Only Memory because nothing can be written into it. This other style of mail-like boxes has instructions that have to remain; it is similar to reading permanent rules from a bulletin board that you must read and follow but cannot change.

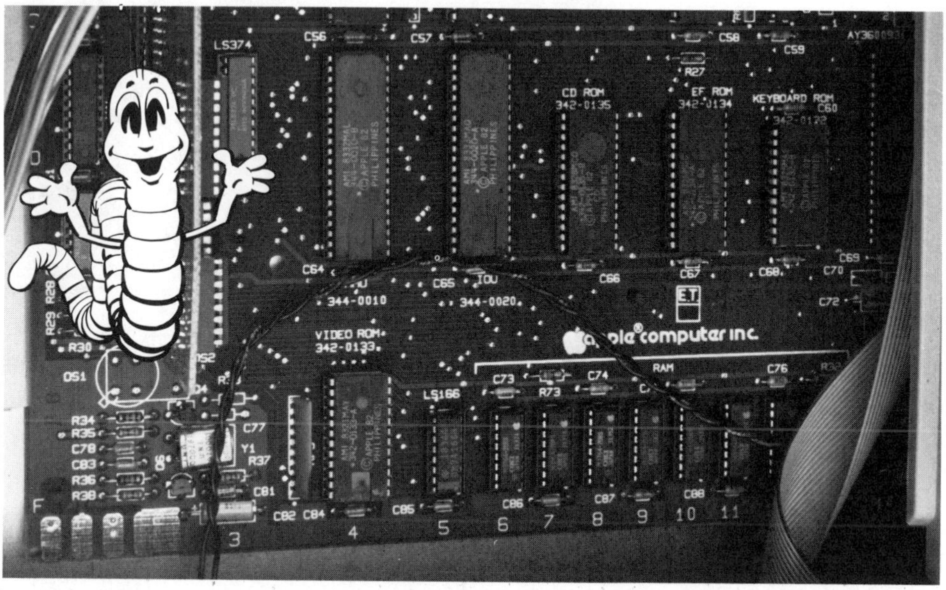

ROM AND RAM MEMORY ARE INSIDE THE COMPUTER.

ROM is permanently programmed with instructions which tell the computer to do operational or work-type functions, such as bringing information from the disk into the main memory of the computer. Instructions stored in ROM are never erased when the computer is turned off. The computer can't work without them!

RAM determines the size of a computer.

The size of a computer is determined by the number of read and write memory chips. The number of chips inserted in a computer to store information in RAM can vary greatly. Circuits are measured by the thousands, or K for short. Therefore, 48 K or kilobytes means that there are approximately 48,000 bytes or places in RAM to store messages. Apple IIe computers come with 64K. The Apple IIc has 128K. Do you know how many K your computer has?

Check in your manual and fill out the following blanks:

My computer has ______K memory which means it has ______bytes.

THE SIZE OF A COMPUTER IS DETERMINED BY RAM.

Computer signals are measured in bits, nibbles, and bytes.

The computer messages or signals are similar to a light being on or off. Have you ever sent a message to a friend by having certain lights turned on or off in your house?

The smallest unit the computer uses is one signal which is called a bit. When four of these are grouped together, they are called a nibble. Now you know how Nibbles got his name. He lives in RAM memory and is made up of bits.

Eight bits make up one byte. These words are computer jargon which you should recognize and remember in order to impress your friends.

4 bits make one nibble.
8 bits make one byte.
48K means the computer has about 48,000 bytes.

BIT IS ONE CIRCUIT...NIBBLE IS FOUR BITS AND BYTE IS EIGHT BITS.

See what's inside the Apple II, Apple II Plus, or Apple IIe.

> **WARNING**: The warranty on an Apple IIc is terminated if the machine is opened! Study a drawing or photo from your book to see the inside sections of your computer. See the note at the bottom of the page.

Take a look inside an Apple II, Plus, or IIe computer to get a better idea of what goes on when you use your computer.

Carefully remove the cover. It pulls up from the back. BE CERTAIN THE MACHINE IS TURNED OFF BEFORE OPENING THE COVER!

Find the large power supply on the left side. Now you know why the large cord plugs in on this side. Now find the memory chips. The ROM memory chips are the larger ones. Can you see them? Now locate the RAM chips which are smaller and more numerous. The processor is easy to spot because it is right in the middle of all the other chips.

Now look for the slots at the back of the computer. The disk drive card is usually placed in the slot marked 6 and the printer is usually inserted in the slot marked 1.

OUCH! LOOK INSIDE. . .BUT DON'T TOUCH!

NOTE: On an Apple IIc, peripherals, such as a printer and disk drive, are inserted into portals at the back of the computer so it isn't necessary to open the computer to insert peripheral connection cards in the slots inside the computer. Please see Chapter 11 for more details.

Study the main sections inside a computer.

Observe carefully and become acquainted with the various parts inside the computer. The computer loses some of its mystery and fearsome qualities when you realize that it is simply a series of electronic parts, very cleverly put together to store electronic impulses or signals.

The disk drive is joined to the computer by a card which is usually placed in Slot #6. The card attached to the printer is usually plugged into Slot #1. These are called interface cards. Can you find yours?

If more than one disk drive is used, two of them may be connected to the same card. How many disk drives do you have?

The large shelf which covers the bottom of the computer and holds all the circuitry is called the motherboard.

Study your computer and compare different sections with pictures in this book and in manuals you received when you bought your computer. If you have some understanding of how a computer works, you'll be more at ease as you use it. You won't have to learn a great deal of technical information . . . just get the general idea of what happens inside the computer.

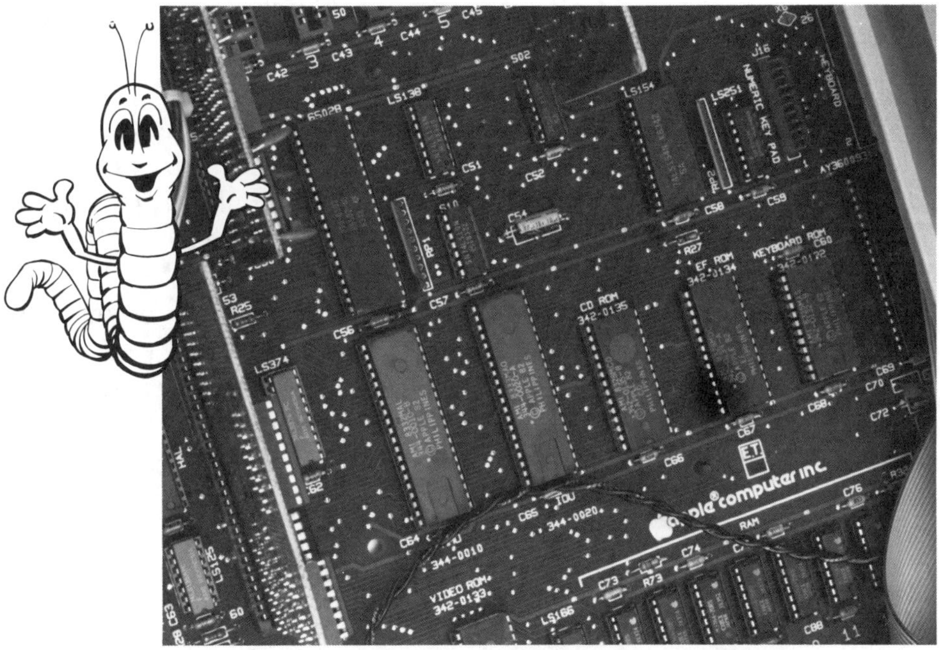

HERE'S A VIEW OF THE MOTHERBOARD.

On the APPLE IIc, the disk drive is inside the computer. A second disk drive may be plugged into the back of the computer. Study Chapter 11 or your manual for more details. Study pictures of your computer or look inside one of the other models. Remember: DON'T TRY TO OPEN THE PORTABLE APPLE IIc!

Hardware deserves good care.

The Apple equipment is sturdy and is user-friendly, which means it won't break if you look at it! However, it is always a good idea to treat equipment with respect and give it the proper care to get the most benefit from it and avoid unnecessary expense. Here are some general rules for taking good care of the equipment:

1. Send in all your warranties properly filled out. Have you done this yet?
2. Read and follow directions very carefully when you assemble any equipment.
3. Don't turn the computer on and off in rapid succession. Count to five when you've turned off the computer and want to turn it back on again.
4. Don't try to type at the same time the disk drive is working. Watch for the red light to go off before typing on the keyboard.
5. Keep the disk drive door closed. Only open it to insert a disk and then close it again.
6. Never open the disk drive door when the red light is on. The red light is a signal to keep hands off!
7. Don't try to open the cover of an Apple IIc portable computer.
8. Turn off the computer before opening the cover of an Apple II, Apple II Plus, or Apple IIe computer.
9. Avoid touching the circuits and electrical components inside any computer.
10. Don't bend the interface cards which are inserted in the slots.

HANDLE YOUR HARDWARE WITH CARE!

VOCABULARY TO REMEMBER

Terms

COMPUTER An electronic machine that can add, subtract, multiply and divide amounts very rapidly and perform other processing operations after receiving coded instructions from a human being.

HARDWARE The main computer equipment which consists of the monitor, keyboard, processor, disk drive or cassette, and printer.

MONITOR A computer output device which looks like a television screen.

PROCESSOR The vital part of the computer which contains the logical, mathematical, and operational circuitry.

KEYBOARD Typewriter-like series of keys used to input coded messages into the processor.

DISK DRIVE A device used to store and retrieve information on disks.

DISK Small phonograph-type storage unit which is used with a disk drive.

AUXILIARY STORAGE Additional storage area outside the main computer memory which is usually on a disk or a tape.

PRINTER A peripheral device that writes information on paper in a readable form.

INPUT Information or data which is sent to the processor to be made more useful.

OUTPUT Information or data which is made more useful after processing.

RAM The read and write memory or random access memory which can be written into as well as read.

ROM The read only memory which is installed when the computer is manufactured. This memory contains operational directions for the computer. Nothing can be written in or added to ROM.

BASIC One of many languages used to communicate with a computer. The letters represent the phrase: Beginner's All-purpose Symbolic Instruction Code.

CREATIVE CORNER

Now it's your turn to do some writing and create some output.

1. Explain how your mind and the computer are similar in the way they function.
2. Why is it important for you to learn about computers?
3. What are some steps to follow to develop a better attitude?
4. What are some uses for the computer?
5. Name the three necessary sections of a computer hardware system.
6. What are some rules to follow to keep the computer in good working order?
7. What is BASIC?
8. What is the difference between ROM and RAM?
9. What is a bit? A nibble? A byte?
10. What does K indicate? What would 128K mean?

Check back in Chapters 1 and 2 if you can't remember some of the answers and need to review.

3
APPLE SOFTWARE DISKS

GOAL: To gain an understanding and working knowledge of software.

THOUGHT: Believe in your ability to learn!

Vocabulary To Learn:

BASIC Commands: RUN CATALOG

TERMS:

SOFTWARE	APPLESOFT BASIC	MENU
WRITE-ENABLE NOTCH	INTEGER BASIC	DIRECTORY (CATALOG)
USER-FRIENDLY	DISK OPERATING SYSTEM (DOS)	INITIALIZE
CURSOR		
PROMPT	BOOT	

Software programs are available to use.

Many excellent **software** programs—the lists of instructions which operate a computer—have been written. Although you can learn to write your own programs, you certainly don't have to work that hard! Using a ready-made program makes it possible to put your computer to work immediately—if you correctly follow directions given in the program.

You can obtain software from many sources. You probably have some software that came with your computer. Perhaps you have a friend who will let you borrow programs. Magazines and books contain hundreds of software programs. Most schools have programs for students to use. Several stores now sell software.

You probably already know that software requires careful handling. Software is expensive; it deserves your proper care.

SOFTWARE TELLS THE COMPUTER WHAT TO DO.

Software disks need proper care.

A disk is made so that information can be stored on its coated surface. The coating is very thin, so the disk must be carefully handled to avoid damaging the surface.

Every disk has a permanent protective covering made of black plastic. Never try to remove this covering to expose the disk inside. The jacket lubricates and protects the disk.

Here are suggestions for protecting your disks.

1. Avoid exposing disks to sun, extreme heat or cold, or moisture.
2. Store disks vertically in their paper envelopes when not in use.
3. Do not bend disks or attach clips to them.
4. Do not erase on the labels. Eraser dust can damage disks.

5. Avoid setting disks on television sets, large motors, or other electronic equipment to prevent disks from being demagnetized.
6. Handle disks by the labels. Don't touch exposed areas.
7. Use only a felt-tip marker when labeling a disk, or prepare the label before attaching it to the disk. Never use a ballpoint pen, fountain pen, pencil or hard marker on the attached label.
8. Avoid eating, drinking, and combing hair around disks, or touching disks with sticky or soiled hands.

Some areas of the disk are not protected by the jacket.

You see only a small part of the disk itself; the jacket which protects the disk has certain important areas which must be cut out to expose the disk surface. Be careful not to touch these areas. There is plenty of covered surface to hold when you must handle a disk. The oils from the skin can ruin the very delicate surface of a disk. Even microscopic dust and smoke can damage a disk. Keep the disks in their envelopes to protect them from all kinds of possible trouble when you are not using them.

The middle area is the spindle hole which allows the disk to be rotated inside the drive. This is similar to the action of a record player. The large oval hole is the section which is read by the disk drive. As the drive rotates the disk, the head moves in a straight line up and down the oval area and reads the magnetic signals. The entire disk can contain messages; however, just the exposed oval area is read at one time. When new material is requested, the disk rotates to another section and new material is exposed in the oval area.

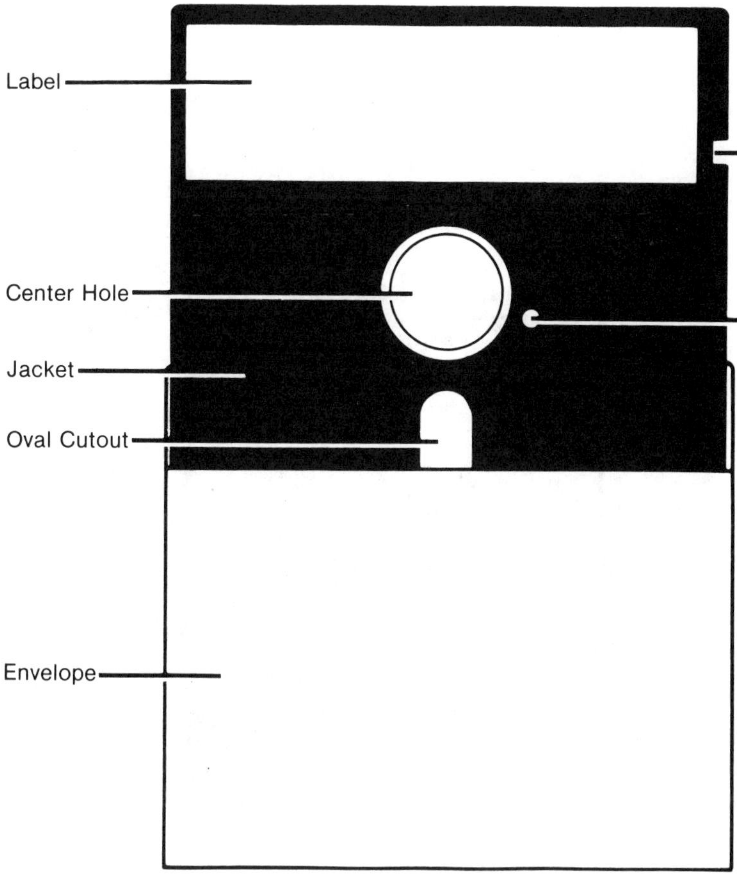

Information can be written on a disk that has a write-enable notch.

The **write-enable** notch is the small square on a disk. This notch allows information to be changed or written. Without the notch, the computer can only read the information; it can't write anything new.

Most professional disks you purchase will be write protected; the write-enable notch will not be on the disk. For example, the disks which come with a new computer usually don't have notches. Check your disks. GETTING DOWN TO BASICS is the only one of the five disks that come with the Apple IIc that has a write-enable notch because you are supposed to add new material to that disk.

Gummed protectors, which come in a package of new disks, can be placed over write-enable notches to make disks write-protected. This protects a program you've written from accidentally being erased or changed.

Disks can be copied.

Some programs are designed to copy material from one disk to another. Some of the disks that come with the Apple IIe or Apple IIc contain copy programs you can use for this purpose. Most commercial software programs have provisions for copying them. It is wise to make an extra copy of a program to use as a backup in case something happens to the original.

It is not ethical, nor legal, to copy a professional program which has been protected by a copyright. Sometimes a program is written so it will erase or "self-destruct" if someone tries to copy it; the original program is removed from the disk so it cannot be used. This is a punishment for trying to copy it. Programmers spend much time developing programs; they should be paid for their work and creativity. Illegal copying is one of the reasons software is expensive. Usually a backup disk is included with a professional disk so it isn't necessary for a beginner to try to copy the original disk.

Now get ready to insert a disk into the drive.

1. Find the APPLE PRESENTS . . . APPLE or another disk of your choice which has a title written on the label.
2. Carefully remove the disk from its paper envelope. Keep this

envelope handy and replace the disk when you are finished.
3. Make certain the computer is turned off. The red light on the disk drive should not be on.
4. Open the disk drive and gently slip the disk into the open slot with the label facing upward.
5. The edge of the disk with the oval cutout should enter the drive first.
6. Close the disk drive door. This places the head in the disk drive so it is ready to read.
7. If you leave a disk in a drive for a long time, open the door so the head is not resting on the disk when it is not being used.

ALWAYS INSERT THE DISK CAREFULLY.

Begin to use the computer!

Now begins the real fun. You are going to turn on the computer and begin to use it. First, make certain the door on the disk drive is closed. It is strongly recommended that a disk be placed in the disk drive before the computer is turned on. In this way, you will have a disk ready to save your work when it's time to turn off the computer.

Turn on the monitor so it can warm up. Now turn on the computer and listen for a beep. The lights on the disk drive and the computer should come on. Do you see them?

LISTEN FOR THE BEEP!

IF you don't have a disk in the disk drive, press the [RESET] key and [CONTROL] key on your keyboard at the same time to stop the disk drive and turn off the red light. The [CONTROL] key is on the left side of the keyboard; the [RESET] is on the upper right. There is a possibility of damaging the drive if it is frequently stopped by using the [CONTROL] [RESET] keys.

NOTE: The Apple IIc is designed to start up with a disk in the drive. A warning message will appear on the screen if there is no disk in the drive as you turn on the computer. If for some reason you don't have a disk, press the [CONTROL] [RESET] keys to clear the screen and get ready to use the keyboard.

On some computers, only the [RESET] needs to be pressed to stop the disk drive. The [CONTROL] key is called [CTRL] on the older Apple II models.

Follow the directions that appear on your screen.

Adjust the monitor so you will be able to see the writing on the screen. Turn the contrast knob to the desired amount of brightness.

Follow the directions on the monitor for whatever program you are using. APPLE PRESENTS . . . APPLE is an excellent program to help you get acquainted with the Apple IIe or IIc. The Apple IIc comes with five excellent disks to teach you some of the things computers can do.

User-friendly programs help you enjoy learning.

All of the Apple demonstration programs are **user-friendly**, which means they try to make the computer-user feel comfortable and not feel frightened or stupid when mistakes are made. Messages or prompts appear when a delay is necessary to let the user know the machine is still working and all is well inside the machine. Some programs are written very rudely, and angrily reply "Wrong," or make a comment which is cold and thoughtless when a mistake is made by the user. Avoid using or writing this type of program.

USER FRIENDLY PROGRAMS ARE POLITE TO YOU.

The cursor shows the next writing position on the screen.

The **cursor** is the signal on the screen used to indicate where the next letters or data will be written.

The cursor is usually square in shape; however, many programs use other shapes or signals to indicate screen location.

Use special keys to start and stop a program.

If you want to stop a program, press the [ESC] key in the upper left corner. (ESC is short for Escape.) If that doesn't work, press the [CONTROL] and [C] keys at the same time. The [C] stands for Cancel. With some programs, you must press [RETURN] after pressing the [CONTROL] and [C] keys.

The [CONTROL] [S] keys can also be used to stop a program. If the [CONTROL] [S] keys are pressed again, the program will continue where it left off. Pressing [CONTROL] [RESET] stops a program, but it might also erase the program in memory.

If this happens, you will have to restart the program.

Software programs differ.

When using a specific program, follow the directions written on the monitor screen or in the written instructions. You will discover that every program has a slightly different set of rules for you to follow. The answer again is to be flexible and try not to become frustrated.

Experiment with various programs, starting and stopping them, until it is easy for you and you feel more like the boss!

FOLLOW SOFTWARE DIRECTIONS.

The prompt indicates the type of language used.

A signal called a **prompt** which may appear on your monitor screen indicates the type of BASIC or other language the program is using. **Applesoft** BASIC and **Integer** BASIC are indicated by the following prompt signals:

] **APPLESOFT** BASIC

> **INTEGER** BASIC

Watch for these language prompts as you run various programs.

If your Apple II or Apple II Plus has a special language card inserted in a slot inside the computer, you will be able to use either Applesoft or Integer BASIC. Most programs are being written in Applesoft today; however, some excellent Integer BASIC programs are still available that you may want to use.

IT'S "BASIC" MY DEAR WATSON!

To change from Applesoft to Integer BASIC, type RUN INTEGER and press the [RETURN] key. To change from Integer to Applesoft BASIC, type FP (which stands for Floating Point) and press the [RETURN] key. The Apple IIc does not use the FP or INTEGER commands.

The message "LANGUAGE NOT AVAILABLE" will appear on your monitor screen if you use a program written in a language that is different from the language indicated by the prompt on the screen. The Apple IIc has a special program on the SYSTEMS UTILITIES disk which checks to see if a disk can be run on the Apple IIc.

What does boot the disk mean?

To **boot** the disk just means getting everything ready to start sending and receiving information back and forth from the disk to the memory. Many new books just say "start up the disk," and don't even bother with the term boot. It originally was called booting the **Disk Operating System** or bootstrapping.

How do you boot or start up a disk?

When the computer is first turned on, the disk drive automatically starts looking for a disk. Try to have a disk in the drive when you turn on your computer. It is easier on the disk drive and gives you the opportunity to save your work on a disk before you turn off the computer.

To restart a disk when the computer is turned on, press the [OPEN-APPLE] and [RESET] keys at the same time, or type PR#6 and press the [RETURN] key. If you are using Integer BASIC, type IN#6 and press the [RETURN] key.

Several Disk Operating Systems are being developed.

Most of the time you won't need to even think about the busy program, commonly called **DOS**, and just let it do its work. However, you should know a little about the different types of systems that are available. You'll want to know how to use these programs to make your work on the computer easier. Your motto should be "Let the program do the pick and shovel work for me!"

The early Apple II computers used a 3.2 Disk Operating System to control the sending of messages back and forth from RAM to the disk drive. Later the improved DOS 3.3 was developed. Now, ProDOS is available for the Apple IIc and IIe and any of the earlier models with extended memory. ProDOS is short for Professional Disk Operating System. Most new Apple programs will be written using ProDOS.

There are three disk operating systems available for the Apple IIc. These are ProDOS, DOS 3.3, and Pascal. Each system saves information on disks in a different way. You must prepare a new disk so that it matches the type of system that is in a program. It is a good idea to keep disks separated according to the type of Disk Operating System used.

Would you like to see the menu?

Some programs have a list of choices from which to choose, called a **menu**. This is similar to a menu found in a restaurant. Using the menu for the SYSTEMS UTILITIES disk, you can select which activity you wish the computer to perform, such as copying or erasing programs on a disk. All it takes is a signal from the keyboard; the program does the rest and runs or brings up what you want.

More and more programs will be written that are menu driven. This means that you will be able to "drive" or control the computer by selecting activities listed in the menu of a program. You won't even have to type very much.

Choices from the menu are made by typing only the number before the selection or using the [UP-ARROW] or [DOWN-ARROW] keys to highlight the chosen section.

Type CATALOG to see the directory (or catalog) on a disk.

When your disk drive has finished booting the disk, you should see a title or information appear on the screen. If there is no menu or any other directions, do the following:

1. Type the command CATALOG (or CAT on the Apple IIc) and press [RETURN]. You should then see a list which is called either the **catalog** or **directory**. The catalog lists the programs that are on the disk. This is similar to opening a file drawer and seeing several titles of folders which are in the drawer.
2. To "pull out" one of the programs "from the drawer" (or select one from the disk), type RUN and the EXACT TITLE listed. Then press the [RETURN] key.

The SYSTEMS UTILITIES disk has a special program listed on its menu called "Identify and Catalog a Disk" which can catalog programs found on other disks.

THAT'S THE ONE I WANT!

A disk can contain several programs; sometimes it is necessary to press [RETURN] to see the complete list. You can tell when you are at the end of the listing when you see the language prompt and the cursor appear.

If you make a mistake as you are typing, use the [←] key to move the cursor back so it's on top of the error; then type the correct letter to replace the mistake. Use the [→] key to retype electronically over characters that are to remain. Use the [RETURN] to start a new line or execute a command. In Chapter 4, there'll be more information about using the keyboard and making corrections.

The catalog gives information about the programs on the disk.

Here is an example of a DOS 3.3 catalog listing of programs on a disk and an explanation of each section. The catalog (directory) is similar to the table of contents of a book. The catalog on your disk may be different from this one; this is just a sample.

```
DISK VOLUME 001
*A  003  HELLO
*I  003  APPLESOFT
*I  026  APPLEVISION
 A  006  BRIAN'S THEME
```

The asterisk (*) indicates that the file is locked and cannot have anything changed or added until it is unlocked. The lock (*) also protects the program from being erased. All of the programs except BRIAN'S THEME on this sample catalog are locked.

The numbers, like 003, indicate the amount of space the program takes up on the disk. These are called "sectors."

LOCKING IS THE KEY TO PROGRAM SAFETY.

The language in which the program is written is indicated by an A for **Applesoft** BASIC, or I for **Integer** BASIC. The name of the program follows. There are other letters such as B for Binary and T for Text which you might find in your catalog listing. Ignore them for now.

Get acquainted with the ProDOS directory.

ProDOS has two types of directory or catalog displays. Here is an example of a 40-column ProDOS disk directory.

```
DIRECTORY:/USER.DISK/
NAME             TYPE   BLOCKS   MODIFIED
*PRODOS          SYS    31       1-JAN-84
*BASIC.SYSTEM    SYS    21       15-NOV-83
*FILER           SYS    51       29-MAR-84
*CONVERT         SYS    42       1-NOV-83
*STARTUP         BAS    3        15-OCT-83
*HYPNOSIS        BAS    3        15-OCT-83
*ANIMALS         BAS    10       15-OCT-83
BLOCKS FREE      88     USED:     192
```

The name of the disk is USER DISK. The asterisks before the names of the programs or files indicate that they are locked or write-protected. The names of the programs are PRODOS, BASIC.SYSTEM, FILER, ETC. Type refers to the kind, or type, of program. For example, SYS is a system type of program that is necessary when using ProDOS.BAS is an Applesoft BASIC language type of program. The last date on which the program was changed or modified is listed after MODIFIED. Blocks refers to how much space on the disks was used to record the program. There are still 88 blocks free and 192 blocks have been used.

The CONVERT program can be used to change programs written in one system to another operating system. For example, a program written in DOS 3.2 can be converted or changed to DOS 3.3 or ProDOS.

The language prompt must match the language of the program.

Be certain the language prompt on your screen matches the language of the program that you choose from the catalog. Remember, A stands for Applesoft BASIC, and the prompt is **]**. I stands for Integer BASIC, and the prompt is >.

Remember that to change from Applesoft (**]**) to Integer (>), you must type INT and press [RETURN]. To change from Integer to Applesoft, type FP, then press [RETURN]. Change to the correct language prompt before you try to RUN a program in either language.

The Apple IIc doesn't have the FP or INTEGER commands. You've learned so much already that you soon will be using software disks just like an expert. Keep practicing using various disks so you'll feel at home using software with your computer.

Make a list of the software you now have; read the directions that come with the programs; write down any special instructions, so you'll have them handy as you use your software.

CHOOSE YOUR SOFTWARE WITH CARE.

Carefully select software.

Before buying a **software** program, ask if you can try it out. Most sale clerks are happy to demonstrate software, so you can make certain you're buying a program you really want and need. Check to see if there is a guarantee before you buy software. This will protect you if something is wrong with the disk or if the program doesn't satisfy your needs after you purchase it.

There are many types of software. The most popular form is called word processing. Using this program, you can write letters, reports, books, etc. Another type of software is called data base. With this, much information can be stored, arranged, and rearranged. Another type is called spreadsheet and is used for math and accounting purposes.

Briefly look through the directions or manuals written for software before you purchase it. If the manual is well-written and understandable, chances are the program itself will be easy to follow and understand.

It is always safer to have a back-up disk for any software you purchase. Some companies supply a second disk as you purchase the original. Some charge an additional fee for the second copy; others allow you to have a copy made for no extra charge. Deal with a local computer supply store that cares about you and will give you the extra service you need. There is a great difference in attention and service . . . so find a place to do business where the clerks make you feel important and you feel comfortable about asking questions and requesting service. You want to get the best software and service you can for your special needs.

Learn to initialize a disk.

To be able to use a brand new disk, it is necessary to **initialize** it or put it in a form so that information can be stored on it. This is known as formatting. After the system has been booted, it is possible to initialize new disks by typing in a program, which is called the Hello or Greeting program.

> **WARNING:** Initializing a disk will erase programs on the disk. Be certain to use a blank disk or a disk you want erased.

Here are the steps to follow:

1. Boot one of the utility disks that came with your computer or use a disk that you know can be used to start up the computer.
2. Type NEW and press [RETURN].
3. Type the following program, or any program you wish, using a line number, the command PRINT in capitals and the message in capitals, surrounded by quotes. This will be explained in Chapter 5.

```
10 PRINT "HELLO"
```

4. Remove the starter disk from the disk drive and insert the new, blank disk if you are using only one disk drive. If you have two drives, you can leave the starter disk in the first drive and place the new disk in the second drive.
5. Type

```
INIT HELLO
```

If you are using two drives, type INIT HELLO, D2.

Press [RETURN]. You will see the red light on the disk drive turn on and will hear the disk drive at work. When the noise stops, and the light goes off, the disk has been initialized.

Software programs, such as ProDOS, make it very easy to initialize. The directions from the program must be followed exactly as they appear on the screen or in the printed instructions. The UTILITIES disk that comes with Apple IIc has an excellent program which can initialize disks. The INIT command is not used with the Apple IIc. The software does all the work.

VOCABULARY TO REMEMBER

BASIC commands

RUN

1. A BASIC command which brings a program from extra storage (such as a disk) to RAM memory.
2. A BASIC command which executes a program.

CATALOG

A BASIC command which brings up the list of programs on a disk to the monitor screen.

Terms

SOFTWARE

The programs which instruct the computer—a set of coded instructions which enable the computer to perform a task.

WRITE-ENABLE NOTCH

A notch on the side of a disk which allows the disk to receive written information.

USER-FRIENDLY	Programs that are supportive, polite, and non-threatening.
CURSOR	Flashing signal on the monitor which indicates where the next writing or action will take place.
PROMPT	Symbol used to indicate program language.
APPLESOFT BASIC	A form of BASIC language used in Apple computers.
INTEGER BASIC	A form of BASIC language used in Apple computers.
DOS	The **Disk Operating System** program that controls the way the computer interacts with the disk drive. ProDOS and DOS 3.3 are two examples of DOS.
BOOT	To load or send the first instructions from a program in the disk drive to RAM memory.
MENU	A list of the available choices of a program.
CATALOG (DIRECTORY)	A list of the programs on a disk.
INITIALIZE	The preparation of a new disk to enable it to store data.

CREATIVE CORNER

Now it's your turn to create some output from what you've learned.

1. What is the difference between software and hardware?
2. What dialect or type of BASIC language is used by the Apple?
3. What is the prompt of this language?
4. What happens when you type CATALOG?
5. Why is the cursor helpful as you type on the computer?
6. What protects a disk from having new material written on it?
7. What does boot mean?
8. What is a menu?
9. What are some of the types of software programs you can purchase?
10. What must be done to a new, empty disk before it is able to store information?
11. What are some suggestions for taking care of software disks?
12. Do you know more about using computer software now than you did before reading this chapter? What have you learned?

Check back in Chapter 3 if you need help on some of the answers. Hardware is discussed in Chapter 2 if you need to review the differences between software and hardware. Hint: hardware is the computer equipment itself and software the programs or instructions to make the hardware equipment work.

4
THE APPLE KEYBOARD

GOAL: To develop efficient keyboarding techniques.

THOUGHT: Experts are beginners who never gave up!

Aa Bb Cc Dd Ee Ff Gg Hh Ii Jj Kk Ll Mm

Vocabulary To Learn:

BASIC Commands: HOME CALL-936

TERMS:

STANDARD (QWERTY) KEYBOARD	HOME ROW	WRAP AROUND
SIMPLIFIED (DVORAK) KEYBOARD	TOUCH TYPING	EDIT MODE

[KEYBOARD KEYS]:

[RETURN]	[SHIFT]	[BACK ARROW] ←
[SPACE BAR]	[REPEAT KEY]	[FORWARD ARROW] →
[CAPS LOCK]		

The keyboard is a very important input device.

The keyboard is the most common method now used to send information to the computer. It is important to learn to use the keyboard with accuracy and speed.

You will type much faster with better accuracy if you follow a few rules:

1. Learn to know the keys by "touch" so you won't have to look at them. This frees you to watch the monitor or the copy as you type. This is similar to playing the piano while looking at the music.
2. Always sit in a proper position at the computer. Keep your back straight and your head erect, feet flat on the floor, elbows relaxed at your sides, wrists low but not touching the computer, fingers curved, and thumbs close together.
3. Develop flexibility in every finger . . .even those little fingers have to be able to move quickly and independently.
4. Keep the hands, arms, elbows, and shoulders quiet.
5. Use the correct finger for each key every time you type. It is worth spending a few hours practicing now to avoid building wrong habits which will be difficult to break later.

I CAN 'PICTURE' YOU USING GOOD TECHNIQUE.

New technology has improved computer keyboards.

Every time new technology advances, computers become faster, more efficient, and easier to operate. The Apple IIc is a good example.

The keyboard of the new Apple IIc is more efficient than the keyboards of earlier Apple models. It is easier to type faster and more accurately on this new keyboard. The key action of the Apple IIc is similar to that of an electric typewriter. The touch and sounds of the keys on the Apple IIc let a typist know when a key has been typed. The soft action found on other keyboards often leads to letters being typed accidentally because the typist can't feel or hear the key action.

Technology is at last making it possible for typists to type at very high speeds. Keyboards are being manufactured which can accept very fast typing without jamming keys together as an image is produced.

The standard keyboard was first designed to slow down typists.

When the first manual typewriters came out in 1873, the inventor first arranged the keys on the keyboard in alphabetic order. Because typists already knew the alphabet, their fingers quickly learned the keys. Typists began to type faster than the typewriters could respond. The key bars which held the letters jammed together as they came up to type on the paper.

The inventor decided to scatter the letters of the alphabet to prevent typists from typing faster than the typewriter could function. This scattered arrangements of letters to reduce speed is the **standard** keyboard, the keyboard most commonly used today on electronic typewriters and computers.

This method is called the standard Sholes or Qwerty keyboard. Sholes is the name of the inventor who patented his typewriter in the 1800s. The Qwerty name comes from the arrangement of the first five letters on the third bank of keys. The invention of the typewriter was an important step towards the development of the computer. Sholes helped make the computer of today a reality.

A simplified keyboard was designed to be more efficient.

A more efficient keyboard was designed in 1936 by a man named Dvorak. The new keyboard was designed to reduce typing fatigue and increase human efficiency. By this time, typewriters had been upgraded to accept faster typing speeds.

The most commonly used letters are placed together on **home row,** which is next to the bottom row. The keyboard is arranged so that neither the left nor the right hand does the bulk of the typing. It is easier to type using alternate hands, which gives a feeling of balance such as in walking. When the letters of a word are typed with only one hand, it slows down a typist.

This **simplified** keyboard is gaining popularity because of the computer industry. The computer is able to accept messages as fast as a typist wants to type. There is no longer a need to slow down typing speeds.

The simplified Dvorak keyboard is available on the Apple IIc.

The Apple IIc is the only personal computer that offers both the **standard** and the **simplified** (Dvorak) keyboard as standard equipment. It just takes a flip of the little switch located above the keyboard to make the necessary internal electronic changes.

The keyboard itself can be changed from a standard to a simplified arrangement. The keys can be popped off and rearranged in new positions. Apple is also making caps to fit over the existing computer keys to change the keyboard from standard to simplified. These caps will eliminate having to remove and reinsert the keyboard keys.

Keyboarding beginners might want to start right out learning the efficient simplified keyboard if they have access to an Apple IIc or a computer with the simplified keyboard.

Standard keyboards will continue to be widely used. Typists who have developed typing skills using the standard keyboard probably won't want to relearn a new keyboard. It is not easy to change habits. However, more and more new computers may feature the simplified keyboard because of the increased speed and efficiency it offers.

The new Computer Generation has a choice of either a standard or simplified keyboard . . . if they use the Apple IIc!

Learning activities will be presented for both types of keyboards.

In this chapter, exercises will be given for both standard and simplified keyboards. First, an exercise will be arranged for the standard keyboard, and then it will be arranged for the simplified. Select the appropriate exercise for you and your computer.

Here is the standard keyboard for the Apple II and II Plus.

The Apple IIe and IIc have special keys added to their keyboards.

There are keys on the Apple IIe and IIc that are not on the Apple II and II Plus; however, the arrangement of the alphabet and numbers on a standard keyboard is the same for all models. Here are keyboards of the Apple IIe and the Apple IIc.

PRESENTING. . .THE APPLE IIe AND IIc STANDARD KEYBOARDS!

These are the home row keys on a STANDARD keyboard.

KEYS:	A	S	D	F	J	K	L	;
FINGERS:	4	3	2	1	1	2	3	4

The little fingers are numbered "4" and the fingers closest to the thumbs are numbered "1."

Place your fingers on the keys as directed above. The thumbs should be pointing straight ahead, almost touching.

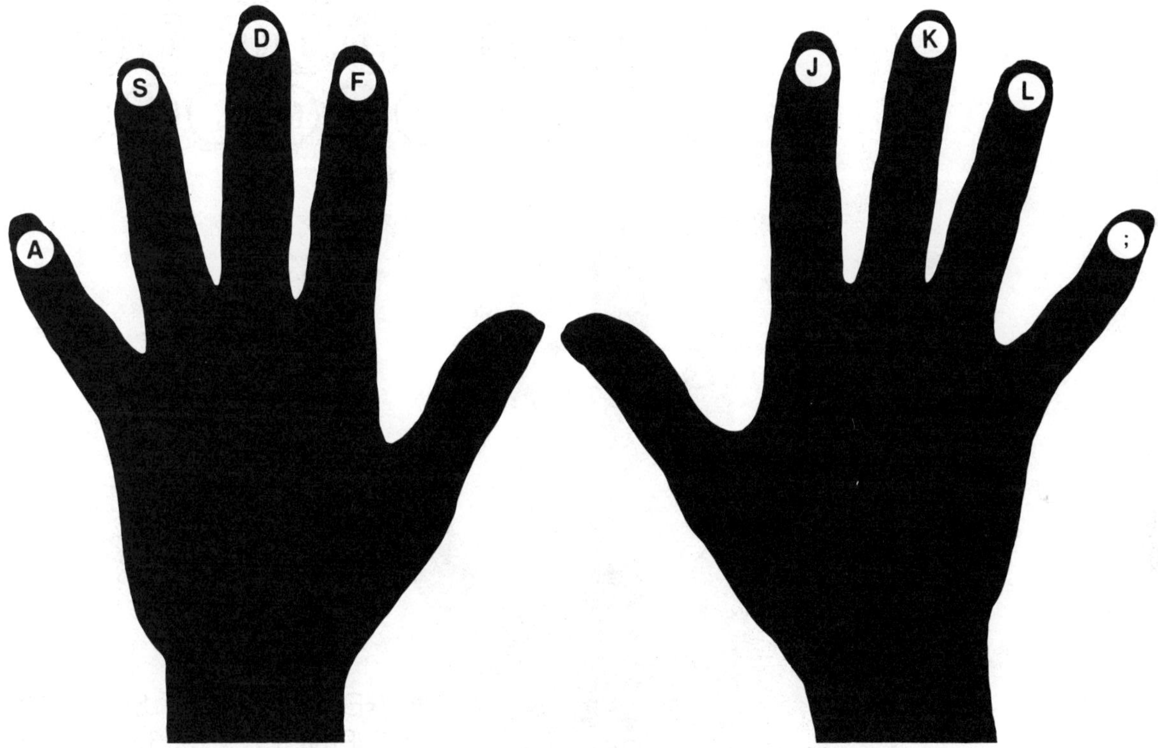

HOME ROW ON THE STANDARD KEYBOARD.

Here is a STANDARD keyboard chart for you to study.

Study this chart and then draw your own chart from memory to make certain you know your keys and correct fingering.

Learn the keys for the LEFT HAND:

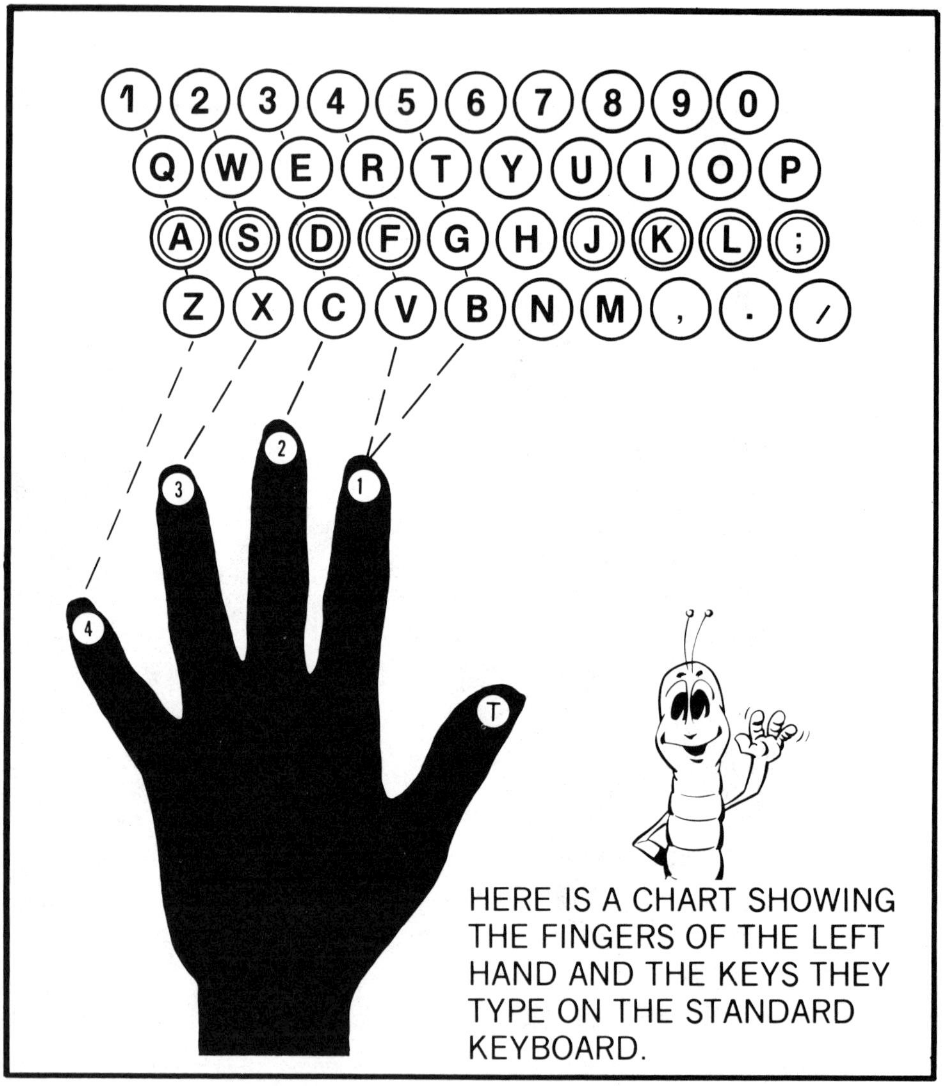

Learn the keys for the right hand on a STANDARD keyboard.

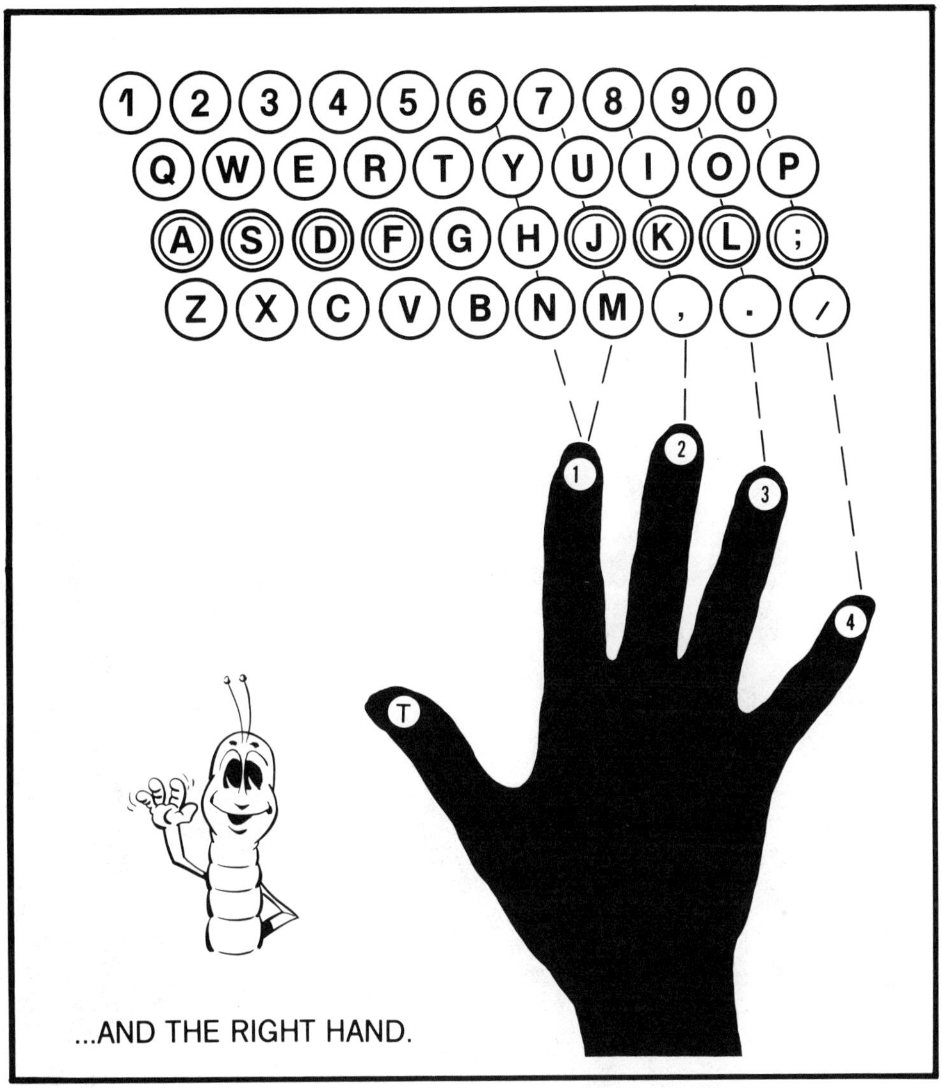

These are the home row keys on the SIMPLIFIED Dvorak keyboard.

KEYS:	A	O	E	U	H	T	N	S
FINGERS:	4	3	2	1	1	2	3	4

Place your fingers on the keys as directed above. The thumb should be pointing straight ahead, almost touching.

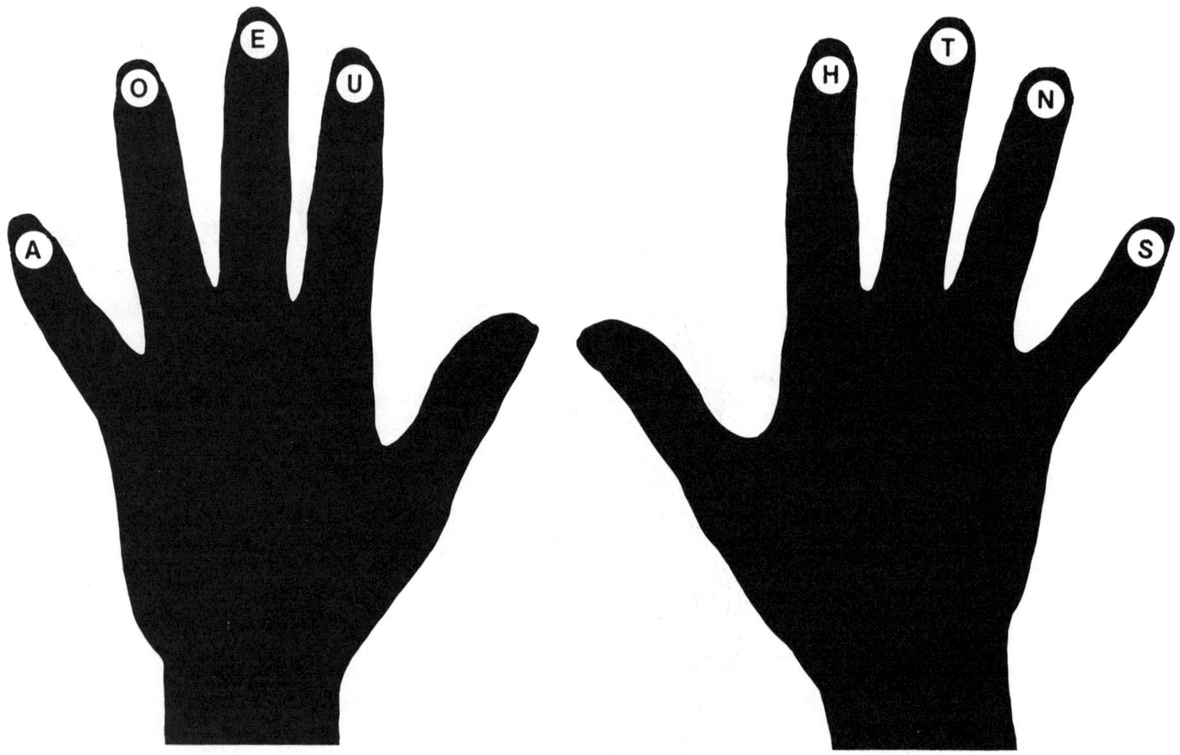

HOME ROW ON THE SIMPLIFIED KEYBOARD.

Here is a SIMPLIFIED keyboard chart for you to study

Study and memorize this chart if you decide to learn to use a simplified keyboard and have an Apple IIc computer. After you have studied this chart, draw it from memory to help you learn the keys and correct fingering.

Learn the keys for the LEFT HAND:

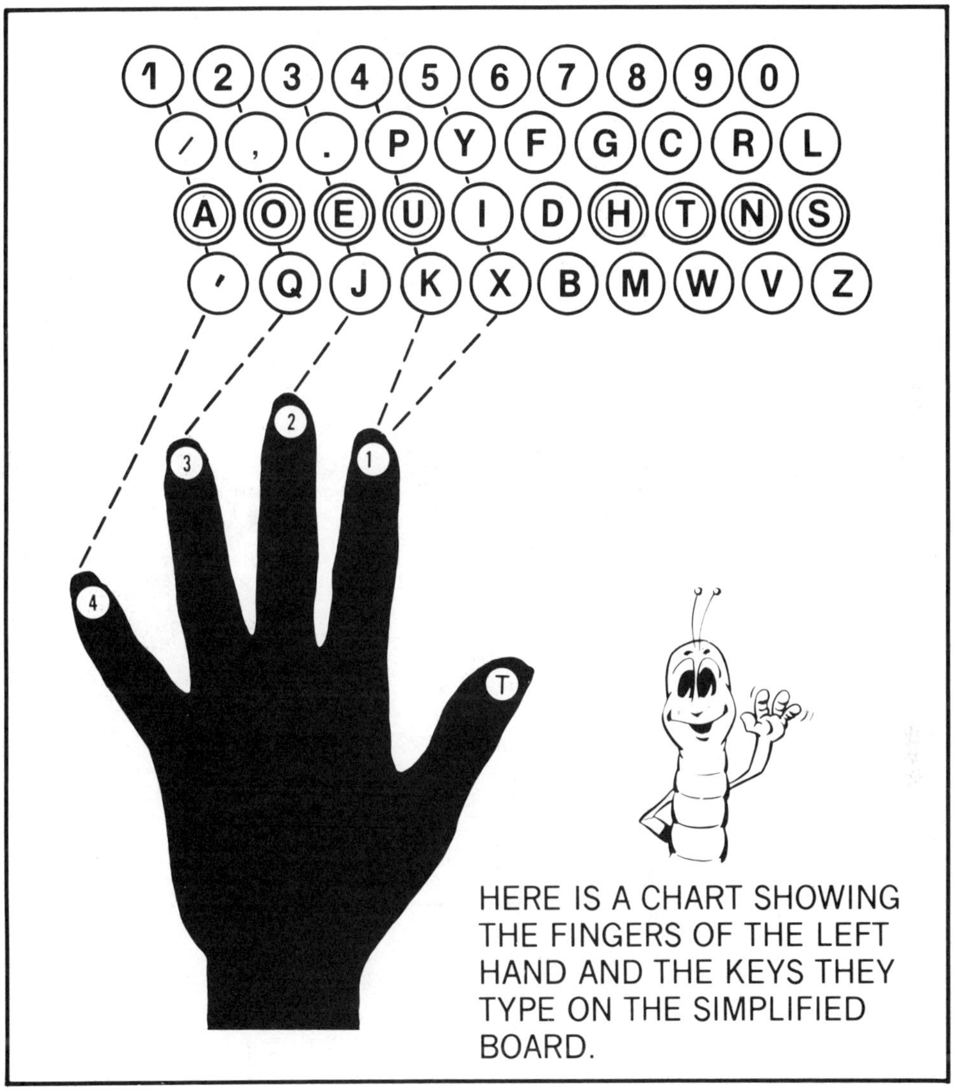

Learn the keys typed with the right hand on a SIMPLIFIED keyboard.

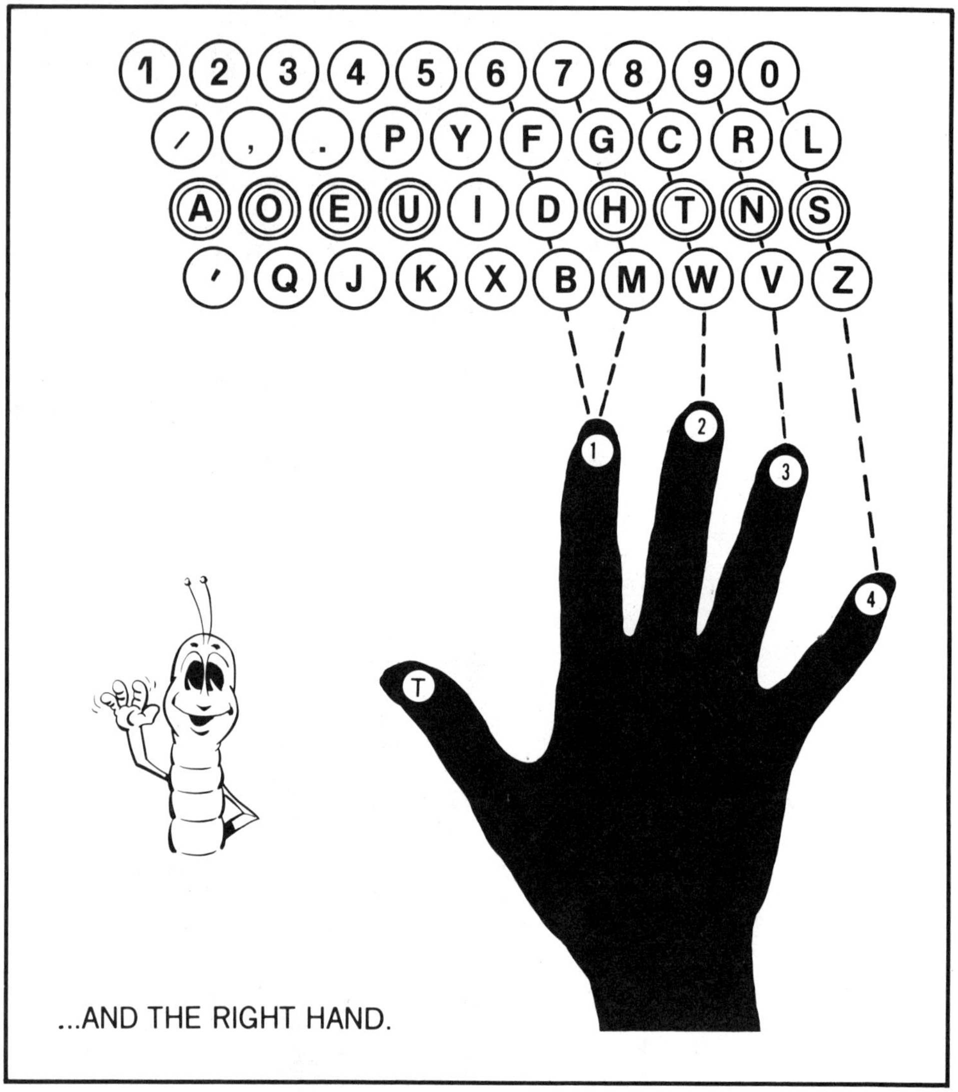

Type the keys on home row.

Turn on your monitor and computer and practice typing the letters on **home row**. The exercises in this chapter are written for both styles of keyboards and are marked **standard** or **simplified**. Select the exercises that match your keyboard arrangement. Use your right thumb to space.

Standard

```
ASDF    JKL;    ASDF    JKL;    ASDF    JKL;
```

(Type these keys several times.)

Simplified

```
AOEU    HTNS    AOEU    HTNS    AOEU    HTNS
```

(Type these keys several times.)

If you don't press [RETURN] when you come to the end of a line, the computer will automatically **WRAP AROUND** to start a new line.

Standard

```
ASDF   JKL;   ASDF   JKL;   ASDF   JKL;   ASDF
ASDF   JKL;   ASDF   JKL;   ASDF   JKL;   ASDF
```

Simplified

```
AOEU   HTNS   AOEU   HTNS   AOEU   HTNS   AOEU
AOEU   HTNS   AOEU   HTNS   AOEU   HTNS   AOEU
```

If you are using an Apple IIe or IIc, press the [CAPS LOCK] located in the lower left corner of the keyboard to make all capital letters. (This is not found on the Apple II or II Plus.)

FOLKS, THESE ARE THE STANDARD AND SIMPLIFIED HOME ROWS.

Keys repeat automatically on an Apple IIe or IIc if they are held down. The keys on the Apple IIe are very sensitive; rest your fingers very lightly on home row to avoid typing characters you don't want.

Ignore syntax errors for now.

Don't let messages that appear on the screen bother you. "SYNTAX ERROR" indicates that the computer doesn't understand the signals you are sending, but it doesn't hurt a thing. Computers are tough so they can survive when a beginner starts using them.

The HOME command clears the screen.

Is your screen getting filled up? To clear the screen first press [RETURN]. Ignore the SYNTAX ERROR and beep sound.

Now type HOME and press [RETURN].

If you are using an Apple with Integer BASIC, type CALL-936 and press [RETURN] to clear the screen. This is the Integer BASIC command that has the same purpose as the HOME command in Applesoft BASIC. If you are using an Apple II, your computer will start up in Integer unless you use an Applesoft language card or are using Applesoft software with your computer.

HOME IS THE BROOM (COMMAND)
THAT SWEEPS THE SCREEN CLEAN.

Your screen should now be clear. If you accidentally typed something other than HOME and pressed [RETURN], the screen will *not* clear. SYNTAX ERROR will appear instead. Just press [RETURN] again and carefully retype HOME. Then press [RETURN]. There . . . did it clear your screen that time?

You can use the [BACK ARROW] on the right side of the keyboard to backspace to correct errors. As you type the correct letter over the incorrect letter, the correct letter will replace the wrong one.

Type HONE, then backspace until you come to N and replace it with M to make it the correct word, HOME.

STANDARD keyboard exercise for keys on the home row.

Move the finger for F over to type G and the J finger over to type H.

```
FGFGFG  JHJHJH  FGFGFG  JHJHJH  FGFGFG  JHJHJH
FGFGFG  JHJHJH  FGFGFG  JHJHJH  FGFGFG  JHJHJH
```

Now type the words:

```
A GLAD DAD HAS A LAD  A GLAD DAD HAS A LAD
A GLAD DAD HAS A LAD  A GLAD DAD HAS A LAD
```

IT'S SILLY, BUT IT'S ON HOME ROW.

Use the [BACK ARROW] to correct errors you make. Ignore the SYNTAX ERROR message when you press [RETURN].

Type HOME and press [RETURN] to clear the screen.

Locate the period (.) which is down from the "L" on the bottom row.

Put in the periods, and you have a sentence!

Space twice after a period at the end of a sentence.

```
A GLAD DAD HAS A LAD.  A GLAD DAD HAS A LAD.
A GLAD DAD HAS A LAD.  A GLAD DAD HAS A LAD.
```

Type HOME and press [RETURN] to clear the screen.

SIMPLIFIED keyboard exercises for keys on home row.

Move the finger that types U over to I and the H finger over to type D.

```
UIUIUI  HDHDHD  UIUIUI  HDHDHD  UIUIUI  HDHDHD
```

Now type the words:

```
TED AND HIS SON HAD SUNTANS
TED AND HIS SON HAD SUNTANS
```

IT'S SILLY ON THE SIMPLIFIED HOME ROW.

Use the [BACK ARROW] to correct errors you make. Ignore the SYNTAX ERROR message when you press [RETURN].

Type HOME and press [RETURN] to clear the screen.

Locate the period (.) which is up from the "E" on the upper row.

Type in the periods, and you have a sentence!

```
TED AND HIS SON HAD SUNTANS.
TED AND HIS SON HAD SUNTANS.
```

Type HOME and press [RETURN] to clear the screen.

Look at a picture or chart of the keyboard as you practice.

The fingers on **home row** move up, down, or over to type the other keys on the keyboard. This exercise should help you to learn the keys on the **standard** keyboard. You may want to prop up a picture or chart of the keyboard you are using so you can look at the chart and not your fingers as you type. This will help you to learn to type by touch . . . and not by peeking!

Try to move just your fingers, not your arms, wrists, or elbows as you type. Keep your right hand in position, and use the right thumb to space.

STANDARD keyboard exercises for the left hand.

Type each line several times to learn these reaches.

Fourth finger (little finger):

```
AQ1QAZ    AQ1QAZ    AQ1QAZ    AQ1QAZ    AQ1QAZ
```

Third finger:

```
SW2WSX    SW2WSX    SW2WSX    SW2WSX    SW2WSX
```

Second finger:

```
DE3EDC    DE3EDC    DE3EDC    DE3EDC    DE3EDC
```

First finger:

```
FR4RFV    FR4RFV    FR4RFV    FR4RFV    FR4RFV
```

First finger:

```
GT5TGB    GT5TGB    GT5TGB    GT5TGB    GT5TGB
```

Remember to type HOME and press [RETURN] to clear your screen.

STANDARD keyboard exercises for the right hand.

Practice these reaches until you learn them. Prop up a picture of the keyboard and begin to look at it instead of your fingers as you type.

Remember to type HOME and press [RETURN] when you wish to clear your screen. Use your right thumb to space. Space five times between sets of characters.

First finger:

```
JU7UJM     JU7UJM     JU7UJM     JU7UJM     JU7UJM
```

First finger:

```
HY6YHN     HY6YHN     HY6YHN     HY6YHN     HY6YHN
```

Second finger:

```
KI8IK,     KI8IK,     KI8IK,     KI8IK,     KI8IK,
```

Third finger:

```
LO9OL.     LO9OL.     LO9OL.     LO9OL.     LO9OL.
```

Fourth finger:

```
;POP;/     ;POP;/     ;POP;/     ;POP;/     ;POP;/
```

This exercise may seem difficult at first, but soon your fingers will reach out automatically.

SIMPLIFIED keyboard exercises to build flexibility.

The fingers on **home row** move up, down, or over to type all the other keys on the **simplified** keyboard. This exercise will teach you most of the keys each home row finger types on the simplified keyboard.

Try to move just your fingers, not your arms, wrists, or elbows as you type. Keep your right hand in position, and use the right thumb to space. Space five times between sets of characters.

Left Hand Exercise:

Type each line several times.

Fourth finger (little finger):

A/1/A'   A/1/A'   A/1/A'   A/1/A'   A/1/A'

Third finger:

O,2,OQ   O,2,OQ   O,2,OQ   O,2,OQ   O,2,OQ

Second finger:

E.3.EJ   E.3.EJ   E.3.EJ   E.3.EJ   E.3.EJ

First finger:

UP4PUK   UP4PUK   UP4PUK   UP4PUK   UP4PUK

First finger:

IY5YIX   IY5YIX   IY5YIX   IY5YIX   IY5YIX

This exercise may seem difficult at first, but soon your fingers will reach out automatically for the correct keys. Remember to type HOME and press [RETURN] to clear the screen.

SIMPLIFIED keyboard exercises for the right hand.

Practice each line several times until your fingers begin to go to the correct keys automatically. Try to keep your arms and hands pointing straight ahead. It may help to look at a chart or picture of the keyboard as you learn these reaches. Try to break away from looking at your fingers as soon as possible.

Type each line several times. Space with your right thumb. Space five times between the groups of characters.

Fourth finger (little finger):

SL0LSZ   SL0SLZ   SL0SLZ   SL0SLZ   SL0SLZ

Third finger:

NR9RNV   NR9RNV   NR9RNV   NR9RNV   NR9RNV

Second finger:

TC8CTW   TC8CTW   TC8CTW   TC8CTW   TC8CTW

First finger:

HG7GHM   HG7GHM   HG7GHM   HG7GHM   HG7GHM

First finger:

DF6FDB   DF6FDB   DF6FDB   DF6FDB   DF6FDB

Soon your fingers will type the correct keys as you see or think a letter or number.

GET THE 'FEEL' OF THE KEYBOARD.

STANDARD keyboard exercise for the upper row of keys.

Here are some easy words for you to type, using letters from **home row** and the upper row on the **standard** keyboard. Type two lines using **wrap around**. Do not press [RETURN]. Let the computer make the new line automatically.

```
WAS   SAG   THE   HIS   SHE   DIG   LET
WAS   SAG   THE   HIS   SHE   DIG   LET

QUE   RED   YOU   PIE   ROW   EAT
QUE   RED   YOU   PIE   ROW   EAT
```

Type HOME and press [RETURN] to clear your screen. Remember, if you are using Integer BASIC, you use CALL-936 to clear the screen.

Type these words with letters from home row and the lower row of keys.

```
ZAZ   SAX   SAC   VAN   BAN   MAN
ZAZ   SAX   SAC   VAN   BAN   MAN
```

Type HOME and press [RETURN] to clear your screen. Notice the cursor goes to the upper left corner of the screen. This is home position for the cursor.

LOOK, YOU DON'T HAVE TO USE THE RETURN KEY.

SIMPLIFIED keyboard exercise for the upper row of keys.

Here are some words to practice on the **home row** and upper bank of the **simplified** keyboard. Type two lines using wrap around. Do not press [RETURN]. Let the computer make the new line automatically. Try to keep your eyes on a keyboard chart or book as you type. Try to avoid constantly looking at your fingers.

```
FED    GOT    LOT    CAT    YET    PET    RIP
FED    GOT    LOT    CAT    YET    PET    RIP
```

Type HOME and press [RETURN] and clear the screen.

Learn the lower row of keys on the SIMPLIFIED keyboard.

Now type these words with letters from HOME ROW and the lower row of keys.

```
JAM    JOX    QUZ    KUZ    VOW    ZEB    MOW
JAM    JOX    QUZ    KUZ    VOW    ZEB    MOW
```

Type HOME and press [RETURN] to clear your screen. Notice that the cursor goes to the upper left corner of the screen for its home position.

Learning to type numbers and symbols on the STANDARD keyboard.

It is very important to learn to type numbers and symbols on a computer. Use the **shift key** when you want to type the symbols located on the number keys. Use the [SHIFT] that is on the opposite side of the keyboard from the key that is to be typed.

Type the following drill. Look at your fingers just at first, then try to keep your eyes on the book. This exercise may be used on the **standard** keyboard for Apple II, II Plus, IIe, and IIc.

Left fourth finger; shift for the !

```
AAA   111   AAA   !!!   AAA   !!!   A1!
AAA   111   AAA   !!!   AAA   !!!   A1!
```

Left third finger; shift for the @.

```
SSS   222   SSS   @@@   SSS   @@@   S2S
SSS   222   SSS   @@@   SSS   @@@   S2S
```

Left second finger; shift for the #.

```
DDD   333   DDD   ###   DDD   ###   D3#
DDD   333   DDD   ###   DDD   ###   D3#
```

Left first finger; shift for the $.

```
FFF   444   FFF   $$$   FFF   $$$   F4F
FFF   444   FFF   $$$   FFF   $$$   F4F
```

FOLLOW MY FINGERS TO THEIR CHARACTERS.

Left first finger; shift for the %.

```
GGG   555   GGG   %%%   GGG   %%%   G5G
GGG   555   GGG   %%%   GGG   %%%   G5G
```

The locations of some of the symbol keys on an Apple II or Apple II Plus differ from this exercise. Study your keyboard to find the exact location of all your symbols.

STANDARD keyboard numbers and symbols typed with the right hand.

Right first finger; shift for ^ (exponentiation).

```
JJJ   666   JJJ   ^^^   JJJ   ^^^   J6J
JJJ   666   JJJ   ^^^   JJJ   ^^^   J6J
```

Right first finger; shift for &.

```
JJJ   777   JJJ   &&&   JJJ   &&&   J7J
JJJ   777   JJJ   &&&   JJJ   &&&   J7J
```

Right second finger; shift for *.

```
KKK   888   KKK   ***   KKK   ***   K8K
KKK   888   KKK   ***   KKK   ***   K8K
```

Right third finger; shift for left parenthesis.

```
lll   999   lll   (((   lll   (((   l9l
lll   999   lll   (((   lll   (((   l9l
```

(Use the lower-case letter L, not the number 1.)

Right fourth finger; shift for right parenthesis.

```
;;;   000   ;;;   )))   ;;;   )))   ;0;
;;;   000   ;;;   )))   ;;;   )))   ;0;
```

(Use the zero, not the letter O.)

Right fourth finger; shift for _ underline.
(Move finger one key to the right on top bank.)

```
;;;   ---   ;;;   ___   ;;;   ___   ;-;
;;;   ---   ;;;   ___   ;;;   ___   ;-;
```

Right fourth finger; shift for + plus sign.
(Move finger two keys to the right on top bank.)

```
;;;   ===   ;;;   +++   ;;;   +++   ;=;
;;;   ===   ;;;   +++   ;;;   +++   ;=;
```

The locations of some of the symbol keys on an Apple II or Apple II Plus differ from this exercise. Study your keyboard to find the exact location of all your symbols.

SIMPLIFIED keyboard numbers and symbols to study.

Numbers and symbols are frequently typed when using a computer; it is necessary to type them with accuracy and speed. Use the **shift key** to type the symbols located on the number keys. Shift with the hand opposite the typing hand.

Type the following drill. Look at your fingers when you first start the exercise to make certain you have the correct locations. Then try to keep your eyes on the book or a keyboard chart as you continue to practice.

Learn more numbers and symbols on the SIMPLIFIED keyboard.

LEFT HAND:
This exercise should be used only on a **simplified** keyboard.

Left fourth finger; shift for the !

```
AAA   111   AAA   !!!   AAA   !!!   A1!
AAA   111   AAA   !!!   AAA   !!!   A1!
```

Left third finger; shift for the @.

```
OOO   222   OOO   @@@   OOO   @@@   O2@
OOO   222   OOO   @@@   OOO   @@@   O2@
```

Left second finger; shift for the #.

```
EEE   333   EEE   ###   EEE   ###   E3#
EEE   333   EEE   ###   EEE   ###   E3#
```

Left first finger; shift for the $.

```
UUU   444   UUU   $$$   UUU   $$$   U4$
UUU   444   UUU   $$$   UUU   $$$   U4$
```

Left first finger; shift for the %.

```
III   555   III   %%%   III   %%%   I5%
III   555   III   %%%   III   %%%   I5%
```

Study your keyboard to see if you have this arrangement.
RIGHT HAND:

Right first finger; shift for ^.

```
DDD   666   DDD   ^^^   DDD   ^^^   D6D
DDD   666   DDD   ^^^   DDD   ^^^   D6D
```

Right first finger; shift for &.

```
HHH   777   HHH   &&&   HHH   &&&   H7H
HHH   777   HHH   &&&   HHH   &&&   H7H
```

Right second finger; shift for *.

```
TTT   888   TTT   ***   TTT   ***   T8T
TTT   888   TTT   ***   TTT   ***   T8T
```

Right third finger; shift for left parenthesis.

```
NNN   999   NNN   (((   NNN   (((   N9N
NNN   999   NNN   (((   NNN   (((   N9N
```

Right fourth finger; shift for right parenthesis.

```
SSS   000   SSS   )))   SSS   )))   S0S
SSS   000   SSS   )))   SSS   )))   S0S
```

Right fourth finger; shift for curved bracket.
(Move finger one key to the right on the top bank.)

```
SSS    [[[    SSS    {{{    SSS    {{{    S[S
SSS    [[[    SSS    {{{    SSS    {{{    S[S
```

Right fourth finger; shift for + plus sign.
(Move finger two keys to the right on the top bank.)

```
SSS    ]]]    SSS    }}}    SSS    }}}    S]S
SSS    ]]]    SSS    }}}    SSS    }}}    S]S
```

Study your keyboard to find the location of all the symbols.

Move your hands to the top bank when typing only numbers.

This exercise may be done on either **standard** or **simplified** keyboards.

When you are typing data containing all numbers and no alphabet, you may place both your hands up on the top bank. This is similar to playing an organ on the top register. Try this exercise with your hands in the upper position. The left hand types 12345 and the right hand types 67890.

```
12345   67890   12345   67890   12345   67890
```

Now type these numbers. Try to keep your eyes on the book!

```
 10   20   30   40   50   60   70   80   90
100  200  300  400  500  600  700  800  900
150  250  350  450  550  650  750  850  950  1050
```

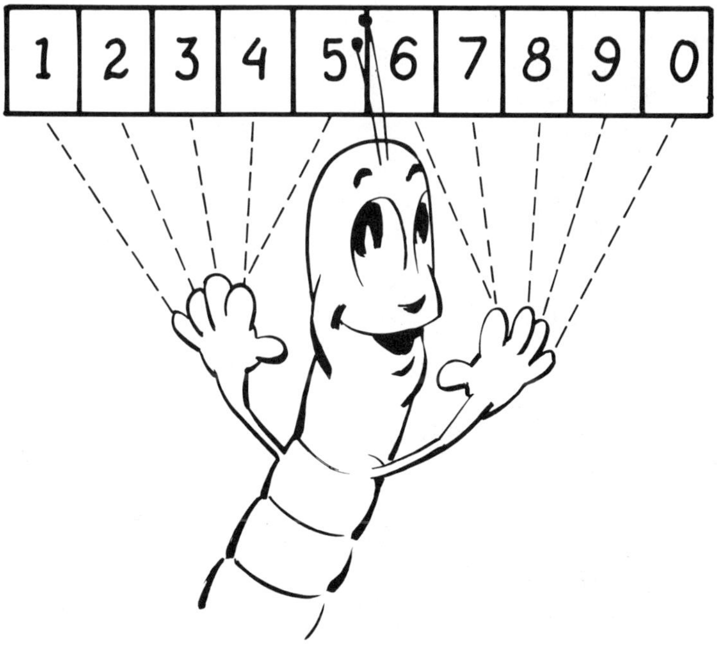

FOLLOW MY FINGERS TO THEIR NUMBERS.

Don't shift and type using the same hand.

Notice that there are two [SHIFT] keys on the keyboard. Remember to use the [SHIFT] key that is opposite the key that is to be capitalized.

Experiment using your [SHIFT] keys to make various symbols. On the Apple IIe and Apple IIc, the [SHIFT] keys can also be used to make the upper and the lower case for the alphabet when the [CAPS LOCK] is in position. You always must shift for symbols, even when the [CAPS LOCK] is down.

Type the following:

```
$4   $4   #3   #3   5%   5%   "HELLO"   (90)   (90)
$4   $4   #3   #3   5%   5%   "HELLO"   (90)   (90)
```

Ignore the "SYNTAX ERROR" if you press [RETURN]. Remember to type HOME and press [RETURN] to clear the screen.

ALWAYS USE TWO HANDS WHEN YOU ARE SHIFTING.

Type math equations using numbers and symbols.

Now type some math equations. Find the addition (+) sign and the equal (=) sign.

```
2+2=4    3+3=6    6+6=12
2+2=4    3+3=6    6+6=12
```

Now find the subtraction (−) sign and type more equations:

```
4-1=3    5-4=1    6-5=1    9-5=4
4-1=3    5-4=1    6-5=1    9-5=4
```

When you learn to use the computer for doing math in Chapter 7, you will find you won't need to type an = (equal sign) in an equation. The computer will do the figuring for you and give you the answer too. For now, become acquainted with the numbers and symbols on the keyboard, using the correct fingers, so you'll be ready for the math in Chapter 7!

Learn the computer math symbols.

The multiplication symbol on the computer is the asterisk (*), which is typed with the left [SHIFT] key held down as the number 8 key is typed. (On the Apple II and Apple II Plus, the asterisk is located next to the zero on the top row.)

The computer doesn't understand if you use "X" for multiplication. Always use "*" instead.

```
4*4=16     3*9=27     5*6=30     8*8=64
4*4=16     3*9=27     5*6=30     8*8=64
```

Type HOME and press [RETURN] to clear the screen.
Use the diagonal (/) key in the lower right to indicate division. (On a **simplified** keyboard, the diagonal (/) key is located above

REMEMBER THE OLD FASHIONED MATH SYMBOLS USED BEFORE COMPUTERS?

4 ÷ 2 = 2

2 × 4 = 8

the A key.) The capital of this key is the question mark (?), which you will use many times in programming.

Type the following division equations:

```
5/5=1     81/9=9     20/5=4     27/9=3
```

There are also symbols on the keyboard which mean greater than, >, and less than, <.

Type the following:

```
5 > 3       8 < 10       100 > 50
```

These expressions have the following meanings:

5 is greater than 3. 8 is less than 10.
100 is greater than 50.

These will be explained more fully in Chapter 7. For now, experiment and type several original math equations to learn the math symbols and the numbers by touch so that you'll be ready to use them in programming.

Learn to type punctuation marks.

Punctuation marks are important in order to make sense out of written communication. You should know how to type punctuation marks by touch and know how many spaces follow each punctuation mark.

Learn to type the period.

The period is typed with the L finger as it moves down to the lower bank. (On a **simplified** keyboard, the period is up from the "E" key.)

`L.L.L.L.L.L.L.L.` (**standard** keyboard)
`E.E.E.E.E.E.E.E.` (**simplified** keyboard)

Learn to space correctly after a period.

Space once after an abbreviation period and twice after a period at the end of a sentence that isn't the end of a line.

Here are examples using the period.

```
Mr. Jones is here.  J. R. Smith is with him.
```

There is one space after the periods following Mr., J., and R. There are two spaces after the period following "here."

Learn to type commas.

On a **standard** keyboard, the comma is typed with the K finger as it moves down to the bottom row. On a **simplified** keyboard, the comma is typed with the O finger as it moves up to the third row.

Space once after a comma when it is used in punctuation. The comma is also used as a command in programming, which will be discussed later. Type the following examples.

```
K,K,K,K,K,K,K,K,K,    ( standard keyboard)
O,O,O,O,O,O,O,O,O,    (simplified keyboard)
```

Here is an example of using commas in a sentence.

```
Bring your books, pencils, and papers.
```

Learn to type the question mark (?).

On the **standard** keyboard, the question mark (?) is typed with the right little finger, down from the semicolon key.

On a **simplified** keyboard, the question mark is typed with the left little finger, up from the "A" key. You must use the [SHIFT] key to print a question mark.

Space twice after a question mark at the end of a sentence if it isn't the end of a line.

Type the following sentences:

Do you like to work on the computer? Are you using correct fingers?

Type the exclamation, parentheses, and the apostrophe symbols.

The exclamation mark is the shift of the number 1 and is typed with the A finger. Space twice after an exclamation.

Here is an example for you to type.

```
A!A!A!A!  !!!!  HURRAY!  HIP HIP HURRAY!
```

The left parenthesis, (, is the shift of 9 and the right parenthesis,), is the shift of 0. Parentheses are used in mathematical equations as well as sentences.

Here are examples for you to type.

```
10 =(20+80)/10
Charlie (who is my boss) is coming!
```

The apostrophe key, ', is next to the semicolon key on Apple IIe and IIc **standard** keyboards. (On the **simplified** keyboards, the apostrophe is down from the A key and is typed with the left little finger.) On Apple II and II Plus keyboards, the apostrophe is the shift of the number 7.

The apostrophe is used to make contractions.

Here are examples for you to type.

```
You'll, I'll, Isn't, He'll, We'll
```

Learn to type a quote.

The quote, ", is the shift of the apostrophe on the Apple IIe and Apple IIc **standard** keyboards. It is the shift of 2 on the Apple II and II Plus. (On the **simplified** keyboard, it is the shift of the apostrophe.)

Here is an example to type.

```
He said, "Come in and see me."
```

"PUNCTUATION IS IMPORTANT! YOU MAY QUOTE ME ON THAT!"

Learn the special keys on the keyboard.

The [RETURN] key is used to indicate the end of a line, and it moves the cursor to the beginning of the next line. Pressing [RETURN] also indicates the end of a command to the computer.

There are four arrow keys on the Apple IIe and IIc and two arrow keys on the Apple II and Apple II Plus.

The [←] and [→] keys are found on all Apple keyboards. The [←] moves the cursor to the left and can be used to erase. The [→] moves the cursor to the right, which electronically types material into the computer as it moves the cursor over characters on the screen. The [↑] and [↓] on the Apple IIe and IIc move the cursor up or down without erasing what is in memory or on the screen.

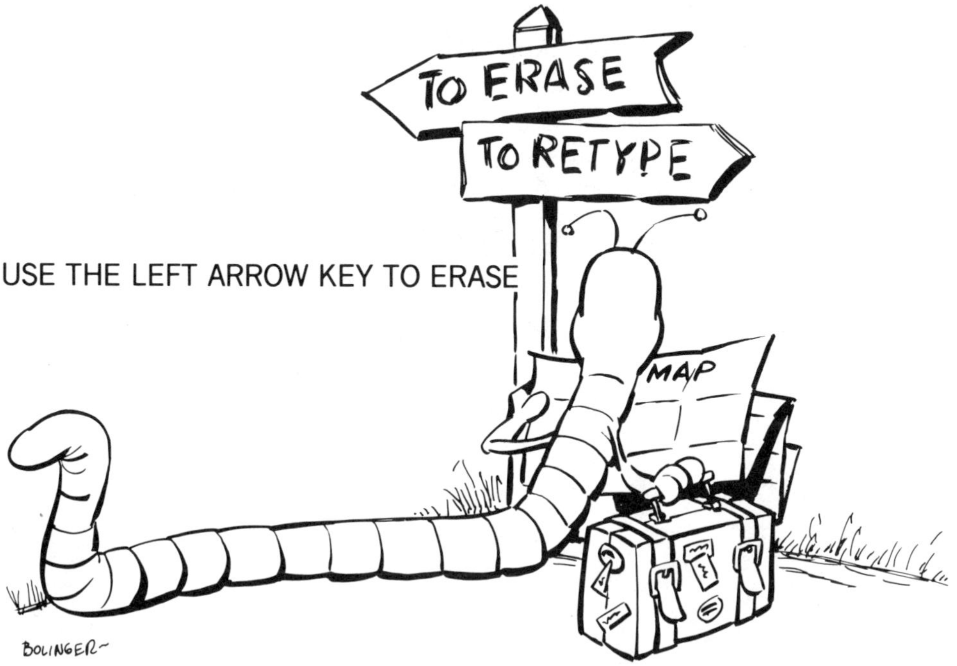

USE THE LEFT ARROW KEY TO ERASE

AND THE RIGHT ARROW KEY TO RETYPE.

The [OPEN Apple] key found on the Apple IIe and Apple IIc has a special function. The [OPEN Apple] is used together with the [CONTROL] [RESET] keys to start up a disk when the computer is already turned on. The [SOLID Apple] found only on the Apple IIe is used to check circuits inside the Apple IIe computer. Hold down the [SOLID Apple] key and press [CONTROL] [RESET]. Release the [CONTROL] [RESET] keys before you release the [SOLID Apple] key. The message "KERNEL OK" will appear on screen if all is well inside Apple IIe.

Learn to repeat . . . repeat . . . repeat.

There is a [REPT] key on the Apple II and Apple II Plus located next to [RETURN]. Hold down the [REPT] before you press any key you wish to repeat. Continue to hold both keys down until you have the desired number of characters. The term "character" refers to any alphabetic, numeric, or symbol used in computers.

The [REPT] is especially helpful when using the [←] or [→] keys. You can really zip across the screen using the [REPT] along with [←] AND [→].

The Apple IIe and IIc have a built-in repeat feature that can be used with any character by holding a key down longer than usual. The key will automatically repeat until you remove your finger.

USE THE REPT KEY TO REPEATTTTT A LETTTTTER.

Use the reset key to stop a program.

The [RESET] key is located at the upper right of the keyboard on an Apple IIe and at the upper left on the Apple IIc. The [RESET] key is used to interrupt or stop a program. It must be used together with the [CTRL] or [CONTROL] key on some computers. The [RESET] is located close to the [RETURN] on the older keyboards and could accidentally be pressed instead of [RETURN]. It is advisable to make a simple adjustment inside the computer which will make it necessary to press both the [CONTROL] and [RESET] keys to interrupt a program. Check your Apple manual for directions or ask your friendly Apple distributor to fix it for you.

Learn to use the other special keys.

The [CONTROL] key, [CTRL], is located on the left side in the center of the keyboard. The [CONTROL] is a non-printing key that is used together with other keys for various functions. [CONTROL] used with [RESET] stops a program. [CTRL] [C] is also used to stop or interrupt a program. There are many other uses of [CONTROL] with various keys. Check your Apple manual and various software manuals for specific directions.

The [ESCAPE], [ESC] key is pressed and released before using another key. Don't continue to hold [ESC] as you use another key. For example, [ESC] is pressed before typing the [K], [I], [J], and [M] keys to move the cursor. The [ESC], with these keys, commands the computer to enter the **edit mode** which is used for making corrections. The [I] key moves the cursor up; [J] moves the cursor to the left; [K] moves the cursor to the right; [M] moves the cursor down. If any other keys are pressed, the edit mode will be interrupted, and the keys will return to their normal work and just print their letters on the screen.

The [TAB] on the Apple IIe and IIc is used to make indentions or columns. This key is used only with certain programs. The [TAB] key cannot be used without the proper software to instruct it.

The [DELETE] key on the Apple IIe and IIc also must be directed by software programs. It is used with word processing software to erase characters.

VOCABULARY TO REMEMBER

BASIC commands

HOME Applesoft command which clears the screen and moves the cursor to the upper left.

CALL −936 Integer command which clears the screen and moves the cursor to the upper left.

Terms

STANDARD (Qwerty) Keyboard The usual arrangement of characters on a keyboard.

SIMPLIFIED (Dvorak) Keyboard An alternate arrangement of the keyboard available on the Apple IIc computer.

HOME ROW The keys on which the fingers rest. (ASDF JKL;) or (AOEU HTNS).

TOUCH TYPING Typing without looking at the keys.

WRAP AROUND The automatic movement of the cursor from the end of one line to the beginning of the next.

EDIT MODE Function in which the [ESC] Key is used with [I], [J], [K], or [M] to move the cursor to make corrections.

Keys

[RETURN] The key used to start a new line or indicate the end of a command.

[SPACE BAR] Bar located at the front of the keyboard used to input spaces between characters.

[CAPS LOCK] Key located on the lower left of the Apple IIe and IIc keyboards which produces all upper case when it is in down position.

[SHIFT] Keys located on lower corners of the keyboard used together with any key to produce an alternate character located on the key. Also used to make capital (upper case) letters.

[REPT] Key on upper right of Apple II or Apple II Plus which repeats any character.

[←] Key which moves the cursor to the left and is used to erase unwanted characters.

[→] Key which moves the cursor to the right and electronically types any character over which it passes.

CREATIVE CORNER

Once again it's your turn to be creative and produce output! Have you learned the material from Chapter 4? Let's find out.

1. Describe good computer keyboard typing techniques.
2. Why is it important to learn to type by touch on the computer?
3. What are the home row keys on your computer keyboard?
4. What symbol is used for multiplication when using a computer?
5. What symbol is used for division when using a computer?
6. Is it necessary to always use [RETURN] to start a new line on a monitor screen?
7. How can you erase one or two letters when typing on a computer?
8. What command is used to clear the screen?
9. What is edit mode? What keys are used with edit mode?
10. What are the two functions of the [RETURN] key?
11. Which model of Apple has a simplified keyboard as well as a standard keyboard arrangement of keys?

5
BEGINNING BASIC PROGRAMMING

GOAL: To write simple programs.

THOUGHT: Learning to master the computer will help me learn to master myself!

Vocabulary To Learn:

BASIC Commands:

PRINT	LIST	IF THEN
RUN	END	GOSUB
NEW	GOTO	RETURN

TERMS:

LITERAL	LINE NUMBER	LOOP
CONSTANT	ASCENDING ORDER	VARIABLE
DELAYED EXECUTION	BRANCHING	

Learn to use the PRINT command with literals.

The PRINT command is used to print characters. When quotes are used with the PRINT command, the characters within the quotes are called a **literal**. The characters will literally be printed the same as they are typed, letter-for-letter.

Type the following example of a literal using capital letters. (Remember, the [CAPS LOCK] on the Apple IIe must be down because the computer reads only capital letters when taking commands. The Apple IIc can take commands in both capital and small letters.)

Type the following:

```
PRINT "LIFE IS A GREAT ADVENTURE!"
   (Press [RETURN])
```

Now you should have a sentence on your screen that says . . .

```
   LIFE IS A GREAT ADVENTURE!
```

THIS IS A 'LITERAL' EXPRESSION.

Numbers in a PRINT statement are called constants.

No quotes are necessary to print numbers with a PRINT command. Numbers in a PRINT statement are called **constants**.

Type the following example of a constant:

Input on Keyboard		Output on Screen
`PRINT 123`	`Press [RETURN].`	`123`

Line numbers store information for delayed execution.

Line numbers store program statements in memory, which is called **delayed execution**. Type the following program with line numbers. Press [RETURN] after each line.

Input on Keyboard	Output on Screen
`10 HOME`	`(Clears screen)`
`20 PRINT "I LIKE NIBBLES"`	`I LIKE NIBBLES`
`30 PRINT "NIBBLES TEACHES ME"`	`NIBBLES TEACHES ME`

Type RUN and press [RETURN]

The RUN command brings a program from memory to output.

The command RUN makes the program go from memory to the processor and then proceed to the screen as output. This is called executing a program.

Now type RUN once more and press [RETURN]. The program will reappear as many times as you type RUN and press [RETURN] because it is still in memory as well as on the screen because of the line numbers and delayed execution.

Delayed execution is very useful.

The real value of a computer comes from its ability to store something in memory then RUN it at a later time. This is called **delayed execution**. (This is similar to storing money in a bank so it can be withdrawn later to make a large purchase.)

Remember, **line numbers** are necessary when using delayed execution. Increments of at least 10 should be used to allow for space between line numbers.

Lines are often numbered 10, 20, 30, 40, etc.

IMMEDIATE EXECUTION

DELAYED EXECUTION

The NEW command erases RAM memory.

The NEW command erases anything from other programs left in RAM memory. It's just like throwing out leftovers from the refrigerator when you bring home new groceries! You don't want to mix in old stuff with new!

If NEW is given a line number, it will erase the new program every time it is run, so don't give NEW a number!

Now type the following lines with line numbers:

Input (Keyboard)	Output (Screen)
`NEW`	
`10 HOME`	`(Clears screen)`
`20 PRINT "I LIKE NIBBLES"`	`I LIKE NIBBLES`
`30  PRINT "NIBBLES TEACHES ME"`	`NIBBLES TEACHES ME`

Type RUN and press [RETURN].

The command RUN starts or executes the program.

Type HOME and press [RETURN] to clear the screen.

The program will run every time you type RUN and press [RETURN] until you erase it by typing NEW and pressing [RETURN].

The computer reads program lines in ascending order.

The computer reads **line numbers** in an **ascending order**, from lowest to highest. Lines may be added that are out of numeric order, but the computer will rearrange them automatically.

Type the data listed under **Input (keyboard)**

Input (keyboard)	**Process or Output**
`NEW`	`(Clears memory)`
`10 HOME`	`(Clears screen)`
`20 PRINT "THE COMPUTER READS CORRECTLY"`	`THE COMPUTER READS CORRECTLY`
`30 PRINT "EVEN WHEN LINES ARE WRITTEN"`	`EVEN WHEN LINES ARE WRITTEN`
`50 PRINT "WRONG ORDER."`	`IN THE`
`40 PRINT "IN THE"`	`WRONG ORDER.`
`RUN (press [RETURN])`	`(Executes the program)`

The LIST command lists the lines of a program in order.

The command LIST instructs the computer to write the list of numbered statements in the program. When the program is listed, it will be in the correct order going from the lowest numbered line to the highest, even though it was written in a different order as it was typed.

Type HOME and press [RETURN]. Now type LIST and press [RETURN]. The computer rearranges the list so it's in the correct order.

Input (Keyboard) **Output (Screen)**

```
LIST          10 HOME
              20 PRINT "THE COMPUTER ALWAYS READS CORRECTLY"
              30 PRINT "EVEN WHEN YOU PUT WORDS"
              40 PRINT "IN THE"
              50 PRINT "WRONG ORDER."
```

ASCENDING FROM LOW TO HIGH

DESCENDING FROM (OUCH!) HIGH TO LOW

Learn to erase or change program lines.

Lines may be erased by typing the line number and pressing [RETURN].

Type the words listed under **Input (keyboard)**. Press [RETURN] after each line.

TYPE THE LINE NUMBER TO ERASE THE WHOLE LINE.

Input (Keyboard)	**Process or Output**
NEW	(Clears memory)
10 HOME	(Clears screen)
20 PRINT "THIS IS FUN"	(Stores in memory)
RUN [RETURN]	THIS IS FUN
LIST [RETURN]	(Displays program)
20	(Erases Line 20)
RUN	(Screen is erased)
LIST	(Line 20 is gone)
20 PRINT "I LIKE THIS"	(Stores in memory)
RUN	I LIKE THIS
LIST	(Lists program with new Line 20)

To change a line, retype the number and add the new characters. The last line entered using the same line number will replace any previous entries at that line number. (See Line 20 above)

Now add another new Line 20:

```
20 PRINT "I CAN CHANGE A PROGRAM LINE."
```

RUN the program, and then LIST the program.

Now write your own Line 20 with PRINT. Just change the sentence that's in quotes.

The question mark (?) is sometimes used in place of PRINT.

The question mark (?) may be used in place of typing the command PRINT. PRINT is the BASIC command; however, the question mark is a shortcut method that takes less time to type. Both the word PRINT and the question mark are called PRINT by the computer in a program listing.

Type the following listed under **Input (Keyboard)**.

Input (Keyboard) **(Explanation)**

```
NEW
10 HOME
20 ? "THIS IS EASY TO TYPE."     (The question mark instead of PRINT)
30 ? "NOW I CAN GO FASTER!"
40 PRINT "THIS TAKES LONGER."    (PRINT is the BASIC command)
50 PRINT "BOTH ARE CORRECT."
```

RUN the program. LIST the program.

The command END indicates the end of a program.

It is advisable to always indicate the end of a program. The command END is used for this purpose. No line numbers larger than the number used for END should be added to a program. Type the following PRINT statements using PRINT and ? (question mark).

```
10 PRINT "LEARN SOMETHING NEW EVERY DAY!"
20 ?  "MAKE UP YOUR MIND TO BE HAPPY!"
30 END
```

Type HOME to clear the screen. Then type RUN to see the program output. Then type LIST to see the list of statements again. (Remember to press [RETURN] at the end of each command.)

Use the semicolon (;) to join lines.

Type a semicolon (;) at the ena of a line in a program to join printing from one line to printing from the following line. When the program is RUN, the computer will be instructed by the semicolon to continue printing on the existing line and not make a new line.

Type the following under **Input (keyboard)**.

Input (keyboard)	**Process**	**Output (Screen)**
HOME	(Clears screen)	
NEW	(Clears memory)	
10 HOME	(Enters memory)	10 HOME
20 PRINT "I ";		20 PRINT "I ";
30 PRINT "LIKE ";		30 PRINT "LIKE ";
40 PRINT "YOU!"		40 PRINT "YOU!"
50 END	(Sets ending)	50 END
LIST	(Prints listing)	
RUN	(Starts program)	I LIKE YOU!

Commas are one method used to make columns on the screen. Type the following listed under **Input (keyboard)**.

Input (keyboard)	**Process**	**Output (Screen)**
NEW	(Clears memory)	
10 HOME	(Clears screen)	
20 PRINT "I","LIKE","YOU!!"		
30 END		
RUN		
		I LIKE YOU!!

The PRINT statement is used to space between lines.

To make blank lines between printed output, type PRINT or question marks (?) in your program listing. They must have program **line numbers**.

Separate commands with a colon.

More than one command can be listed after a **line number** when separated by a colon (:). Notice in Line 30 the two PRINT commands using the same line number; they are separated by a colon. Each PRINT will print one blank line, making a double-spaced effect. Notice that the question mark (?) can be used as a substitute for the word PRINT. See Lines 20, 40, 45, and 50.

Type the following under **Input (keyboard)**.

Input (keyboard)	Process	Output
NEW	(Clears memory)	
10 HOME	(Clears screen)	
20 ?"I KNOW MORE TODAY" 30 PRINT:PRINT	(Prints two blank lines)	
40 ?"THAN I DID" 50 ?"YESTERDAY!" 60 END	(Sets ending of program)	
RUN	(Starts program)	I KNOW MORE TODAY
45 ?:?	(Prints two blank lines)	THAN I DID YESTERDAY!
RUN	(Starts program again)	I KNOW MORE TODAY THAN I DID YESTERDAY!

(Remember to press [RETURN] at the end of each command.)

Computers can repeat an action in a program.

Computers are able to repeat an action very rapidly. This ability is one of the great advantages of using a computer. A computer can read a line and perform an action, and then go back and reread the line and repeat the action. This is called a **loop**. It's similar to a ferris wheel or a merry-go-round repeating a circular pattern, returning to the same spot each time.

GOTO is a **loop** command. Type the following program to see how a loop can repeat and repeat . . . and repeat . . . .

Input (Keyboard)	**Process or Output**
`NEW`	
`10 HOME`	
`20 ?"I'M RUNNING AFTER NIBBLES."`	`(A screenful of I'M RUNNING AFTER NIBBLES.)`
`30 GOTO 20`	`(Returns to line 20)`

A LOOP IS LIKE A FERRIS WHEEL.

Type RUN and press [RETURN] to run the program.

(Press [CONTROL] [C] to stop the loop when you're tired of running!)

Now add a GOTO line to another program from this chapter:

```
NEW
10 HOME
20 ? "LIFE IS A GREAT ADVENTURE!"
30 GOTO 20
```

Type RUN and press [RETURN].

The computer can really take off like a runaway horse when it gets in an endless loop, so you'll have to "pull in the reins" by pressing [CONTROL] [C] to stop the runaway!

Use GOTO to repeat an action.

Have you ever been told to write a sentence or a word 100 times? Parents and teachers sometimes use this method to teach a particular lesson.

Shhhh. . . . I'm going to show you a computer program that will help do this tedious type of assignment very quickly and painlessly!

The GOTO command that you just learned, can be used to write your lesson the next time you must repeat something many times.

Study and type the following:

```
NEW
10 HOME
20 PRINT "I WILL BE POLITE!"
30 GOTO 20                    (The computer is
                              told to go to
                              Line 20 and write
                              the line again.)
```

Type RUN and press [RETURN] to see how your screen will be filled with the sentence. In fact, it will be so filled, you'd better press [CONTROL] [C] or [CONTROL] [RESET] to stop the computer.

THIS IS THE EASY WAY TO SAY SOMETHING 100 TIMES.

(In Lesson 7, there are instructions telling how to print this and other programs on a printer.)

GOTO commands are unconditional branch commands.

The GOTO command is called an **unconditional branch**, which means the computer has to keep going back to a certain line to repeat what is to be written or done, with no exceptions. This is similar to when someone in your childhood told you, "Go to your room!" You were told to "GOTO" your room without delay or discussion; you were to stay in your room until you received further instructions!

With the GOTO command, you can send the computer to a certain line and make it stay there until you tell it to "come out" and do something else. You can be the boss! Enjoy the feeling of power as you learn to control the computer—and yourself, too!

Study and type this program:

```
NEW
10 HOME
20 PRINT "I WILL TREAT OTHERS ";
25 PRINT "THE WAY I LIKE TO BE TREATED."
30 GOTO 20
```

Type RUN and press [RETURN].

Be ready to press [CONTROL] and [C] to stop the computer from the GOTO **loop**.

"GOTO" LINE 20 'TIL I TELL YOU TO STOP.

A counter is a variable that counts repeated actions.

A counter is used with the GOTO loops to count the number of times something is repeated. A counter is one type of **variable**. Variables are symbols that represent values that can change. Variables are necessary in making **loops**.

First, the variable is set at zero, representing that no loops have occurred. Then after each pass or repetition of the loop, the counter is automatically increased by one.

In algebra, a variable is usually a single alphabetic letter, such as X, Y, or Z; but in BASIC, a variable can be several letters long or be a combination of letters and numbers. A counter variable is often named COUNT or COUNTER or just C in a BASIC program.

Using a counter, or counting repetitions, happens frequently in everyday activities. To make cookies, a person usually follows a recipe. When a cookie recipe reads, "Beat the mixture 30 strokes," the cook starts with zero strokes. One stir around the bowl would be equal to zero plus one, which would be one stroke; the next stroke would be one stroke plus one more, which would make two strokes; the next stroke would be two strokes plus one more, equaling three strokes; and so on, counting up to 30—each time adding one more stroke until 30 is reached. When the counting and mixing are completed, the cook would then GOTO the next line of the recipe to see the next steps to follow.

THIRTY STROKES, THEN "GOTO" THE OVEN.

The IF THEN command can be used with GOTO to stop a loop.

When there is a counter in a program with a GOTO statement, the computer has a limit placed on the number of times it loops.

The IF THEN statement may be used in a program with a counter and a GOTO. The computer is told IF the action or work is finished, THEN the computer should GOTO another line in the program.

Here are some examples for you to study and type:

Input (Keyboard)	Process
NEW	(Memory is cleared.)
10 HOME	(Screen is cleared.)
20 C = 0	(A VARIABLE given the name C is set.)
30 PRINT "I WILL BE POLITE."	
40 C = C + 1	(Each time the sentence is printed, the VARIABLE C is assigned one number higher. C = 0 + 1 so now the VARIABLE, still called C, equals 1; one sentence has been printed.)
50 IF C = 20 THEN GOTO 80	(If C = 20, the sentence has been printed 20 times; the computer goes to Line 80, skipping Line 70.)
70 GOTO 40	(Because C doesn't equal 20 yet, the sentence hasn't been printed 20 times. The computer is told to GOTO Line 40 and print the sentence again.)
80 END	(That's all, folks!)

Type RUN and press [RETURN]. Now you won't have the computer acting like a runaway horse! The computer will only print 20 lines.

The GOSUB statement is used to branch to other areas of the program.

GOSUB is similar to the GOTO command. Both commands are used to instruct the computer to make an **unconditional branch**. GOSUB is used with the command, RETURN. With GOSUB the computer is told to go, or branch, to a line that is not next in regular **ascending** order. When the computer has completed the task at the line to which it was directed and then reads the RETURN command, the computer returns back to the line following the GOSUB command to find the next instruction.

Study carefully, then type and run the following program. Notice how the computer can return back to the lines following the GOSUB when the command RETURN is given.

```
NEW
10 HOME
20 REM PRINT A
25 GOSUB 100             (Goes to line 100)
30 REM PRINT P
35 GOSUB 200             (Goes to line 200)
40 REM PRINT P
50 GOSUB 250             (Goes to line 250)
60 REM PRINT L
65 GOSUB 270             (Goes to line 270)
70 REM PRINT E
75 GOSUB 280             (Goes to line 280)

80 END                   (Terminates the
                         program)
100 PRINT "A"            (Prints the letter A)
120 RETURN               (Will return to line
                         30)
200 PRINT "P"            (Prints the letter P)
240 RETURN               (Will return to line
                         40)

250 PRINT "P"            (Prints the letter P)
260 RETURN               (Will return to line
                         60)
270 PRINT "L"            (Prints the letter L)
275 RETURN               (Will return to line
                         70)
280 PRINT "E"            (Prints the letter E)
285 RETURN               (Will return to
                         line 80 and End)
```

Type RUN press [RETURN] to see the program.

VOCABULARY TO REMEMBER

BASIC commands

PRINT	Command used to print words, numbers, and symbols. Also used for spacing between lines.
RUN	Command to execute or start a program.
NEW	Command which erases everything in memory.
LIST	Command that lists the program lines.
END	Command which designates the last line of a program.
GOTO	Command to return or progress to a line number which is out of ascending order.
IF THEN	A command used to make a decision, which determines the action to follow next.
GOSUB	Command to progress to a line number which is out of ascending order.
RETURN	Used with the GOSUB command to return to the line following the GOSUB command.

Terms

LITERAL	Any letters, numbers, or symbols enclosed within quotation marks (") that are printed.
CONSTANT	Characters that are printed without quotation marks.
DELAYED EXECUTION	The storing of program lines in memory.
LINE NUMBER	Number that identifies a program line.
ASCENDING ORDER	Reading numbers from the lowest to highest.
BRANCHING	Breaking away from the usual ascending order of reading line numbers and going to another section of the program listing.
LOOP	Program lines that may be repeated more than once.
VARIABLE	Symbols that represent changeable amounts.

CREATIVE CORNER

Now it's time to write your first programs. Check back in this chapter if you need to review. (There are "hints" to help you on this page too.)

1. First write a program that will print your name just once in immediate execution. Use PRINT and quotations.

2. Now change the program into delayed execution by adding a line number. Add another line to make it repeat in a loop.
   (Hint: Use the GOTO command. Press [CONTROL] [C] to stop the loop.)
3. PRINT three friends' names and phone numbers in two columns.
   (Here is an example . . . change the names and numbers so they are people you know and call.)

```
HOME
NEW
10 HOME
20 PRINT "SALLY", "944-5533"
30 PRINT "JOE", "932-5566"
40 PRINT "MARY","832-9832"
50 END
```

4. Add line numbers 25 and 35 to double space your program. (Hint: Remember the command PRINT is used to make blank spaces.)

```
25 PRINT
35 PRINT
```

Study these programs and predict the output on a computer.

Review some of the exciting new things you've learned about programming in this chapter. Predict what will appear on the screen when you RUN the program.

```
NEW
10 HOME
20 PRINT "PROGRAMMING REQUIRES THINKING."
30 PRINT:PRINT
40 PRINT "IT'S EXCITING TO LEARN NEW THINGS."
50 END
```

(Review the chapter if you need to recheck some commands.)

Predict what will appear on the screen in this next program. In what order will it be arranged?

```
NEW
10 HOME
40 PRINT "ENJOY WORK"
20 ? "EVERYONE SHOULD LEARN"
30 PRINT "TO"
50 END
```

Now type both programs and RUN them to see if you were correct in your predictions.

6
BASIC PROGRAMMING

GOAL: To learn to use BASIC programming commands.

THOUGHT: Learn to be a problem solver!

Vocabulary To Learn:

BASIC Commands:

REM	INVERSE	SPEED =
HTAB	NORMAL	SAVE
VTAB	FLASH	LOAD
PRINT TAB	FOR-NEXT	

TERMS:

DOCUMENT	PROGRAM DESIGN
STRING VARIABLE	SCREEN SPACING CHART

Use REM statements to document programs.

It is important to learn to write programs that are understandable. The REM statement is used to **document** or make comments about a program. The REM statement shows only when a program is listed, not when a program is RUN. REM statements may be used to give the title of the program, the date it was written, the programmer's name, explanations of various sections of the program which follow, etc. REM is sometimes called remark. Quotes are not used with REM as they are with PRINT.

Type the following lines:

Input

```
NEW
10 HOME
20 REM MY FIRST PROGRAM
30 REM WRITTEN MARCH 1
40 PRINT "I CAN SOLVE PROBLEMS."
50 END
```

Output

```
I CAN SOLVE PROBLEMS
```

(Type RUN to see the output. Now type LIST. Notice REM appears only when you type LIST.)

Learn to arrange output on the screen.

Certain BASIC commands are used to "pretty up" output on the screen. Just as the message on a greeting card may be centered, words on the computer screen may be arranged attractively.

IT'S NICE TO "PRETTY UP" THE OUTPUT.

The command HTAB, which means horizontal tab, is used to center material horizontally, across the screen; and VTAB, which means vertical tab, is used to center vertically, up and down.

Learn the size of the screen.

The screen has 40 spaces across, horizontally, and 24 lines up and down, vertically. The computer will scroll or roll up characters on the screen to make room for new material if more than 23 lines are to be printed. Even though the first lines won't be on the screen, they will be in memory. The following program allows everything to be on the screen at the same time.

Type the following:

```
NEW
10 HOME
20 ?"THIS IS THE TOP LINE."
25 VTAB 12
30 ?"THERE ARE 24 VERTICAL LINES ON THE
   SCREEN."
40 VTAB 23: ?"THIS IS THE BOTTOM LINE."
50 END
```

RUN the program. LIST the program.

The screen has 40 horizontal spaces.

Type the following:

```
10 HOME
20 HTAB 11
30 ?"HORIZONTAL PLACEMENT"
40 HTAB 2:VTAB 8
50 ?"THERE ARE 40 SPACES ACROSS THE
   SCREEN."
60 END
```

RUN the program. LIST the program.

Use the PRINT TAB statement to make columns.

PRINT TAB may be used to tabulate or make columns. The desired number of spaces is placed in parentheses following TAB. Type a semicolon after the final parenthesis, separating it from the literal that is to be printed.

Type the following:

```
NEW
10 HOME
20 PRINT TAB (10); "HELLO"
30 PRINT TAB (20); "HELLO"
40 PRINT TAB (30); "HELLO"
50 END
```

RUN the program.

LIST the program.

Add semicolons (;) to the ends of lines 20 and 30. Now the three "HELLOs" will be printed on one line. Semicolons prevent the computer from printing on the next line.

Use INVERSE to emphasize important information on the screen.

The INVERSE command reverses the colors on the screen. The NORMAL lighting arrangement of a black background with light characters is reversed to a light background with dark characters. The FLASH command flashes screen output on and off. Both the INVERSE and FLASH commands are used only with a monitor. Do not use this command when using a printer as output.

Do not try to add program lines to a listing while in the inverse mode if you are using an Apple II, II Plus or IIe. Type NORMAL before you try to write new program lines. (The Apple IIc has been designed so that program lines can be added in INVERSE.)

Now type the following to see horizontal placement, INVERSE, FLASH, and NORMAL commands at work:

```
NEW
10 HOME
20 VTAB 5: HTAB 14
30 FLASH
40 PRINT "THIS IS FANCY!"
50 VTAB 10:HTAB 14
60 NORMAL
70 PRINT "THIS IS NORMAL"
80 END
```

RUN the program.

Now type this program:

```
NEW
10 HOME
20 INVERSE
30 VTAB 5:HTAB 5
40 PRINT "THIS IS INVERSE."
50 NORMAL
60 VTAB 10:HTAB 8
70 PRINT "NOW IT'S NORMAL AGAIN"
80 END
```

RUN the program. LIST if desired.

The rate of screen output can be reduced.

Another way to make the screen easier to read is to delay or slow down the rate at which writing appears on the screen. FOR-NEXT is a command used to delay an action by having the computer count a specific number of times before going to the next line.

Here is an example of a FOR-NEXT delay loop:

```
FOR X = 1 TO 1000: NEXT X
```

The computer will count from 1 to 1000. Whatever is on the screen will remain until the computer reaches 1000 (or any other desired amount). The next line will appear after the computer finishes counting, so it gives a delayed printing effect. The computer counts very fast so it doesn't take very long!

Type the following to see how the FOR-NEXT delay loop affects a program:

```
NEW
10 REM USE FOR-NEXT DELAY LOOPS
15 HOME
20 PRINT "A DELAY LOOP"
30 FOR X = 1 TO 1000:NEXT X
40 PRINT "INSTRUCTS A COMPUTER"
50 PRINT "TO COUNT."
60 END
```

HOLD THAT POSE 'TIL I COUNT TO 1000.

Now stop and check to make certain you have everything exactly as it is in the program. Now RUN the program.

SPEED is another command that will slow down output. The usual SPEED of output is 255. If you type SPEED = 100 or any amount less than 255, it will slow down output. This is discussed more fully in Chapter 9.

Check your program for type errors if it won't run.

Did your program run? If not, check for the following "bugs" or possible errors in typing the program.

1. Did you type the quotes for the literals in the PRINT statements in Lines 20 and 40?
2. Did you type small letter L's or capital O's in Line 30 or for any of the line numbers, instead of using 1's and 0's (zeros)?
3. Do you have the colon (:) before NEXT in Line 30?
4. Did you spell REM and HOME correctly in Lines 10 and 15?
5. Did you use all capital letters (if you use an Apple IIe)?

Learn to be an expert proofreader.

Try to find your mistakes and correct them before your run a program. Develop good techniques so you'll type with both accuracy and speed. Remember, you can use [←] to backspace to make a correction if the cursor is on the same line as the error.

LEARN TO BE A GOOD PROOFREADER.

Retype lines at the bottom of the program if the lines are above the cursor, making them difficult to correct in the usual [←] backspace method. The computer will automatically place the lines in their correct positions according to their line numbers.

FOR-NEXT is used for making loops to repeat an action.

The FOR-NEXT loop which was used as a time delay in this chapter is similar to the GOTO loops in Chapter 5. However, all FOR-NEXT loops have the advantage of having a built-in counter. For example, any variable following the FOR command acts as a counter and adds up the number of times the computer loops back and forth from the NEXT statement to the FOR statement.

Here is an explanation of the FOR-NEXT time delay loop from this chapter: (FOR X = 1 TO 1000 : NEXT X).

First, the X is assigned the value 1; then each time the NEXT statement is read, the X is automatically increased by one. X is going to equal every value between 1 and 1000 before the loop is finished. The computer loops back and forth from the FOR statement to the NEXT statement until the upper limit, 1000, is reached. The computer will then stop looping and go to the line following NEXT in the program instead of looping back to FOR. The loop has been completed 1000 times. Lines following the FOR-NEXT delay loop are delayed until the looping is completed. The computer goes very fast so it doesn't take long to do something 1000 times!

Any variable can be used with FOR-NEXT. It doesn't have to be X. And the number of loops doesn't have to be 1000. Change the number following TO to any amount of loops you want.

Variables are an important part of programming.

Remember variables are symbols that stand for amounts that can change and become greater or smaller in value. Variables make looping and repeating on a computer possible. They are a very necessary part of writing programs, so it is important to know the correct method of using them.

BASIC commands cannot be used as variables.

Variables may be made up of several letters and may even be recognizable words. Words or any combination of letters must never contain exact parts of any BASIC commands. When a computer reads a command used as a variable, it gets confused. The words or letters saved for BASIC commands only are called reserved words. These words are listed in the back of this book. VARIABLES MUST BEGIN WITH AN ALPHABETIC CHARACTER.

Numbers, symbols, or letters may follow the first letter; however a variable can never begin with a number or a symbol.

Here are examples of acceptable variables:

X	NAME
X5	NUMBER
XA3	BK#

Here are incorrect variables:

PRICE	(PR is reserved for PR#6 and others.)
TOTAL	(TO is reserved for TO with FOR NEXT)
9BB	(Cannot begin with a number)

Variables are similar to players on a baseball team!

If a girl named SALLY starts out on a team as a pitcher, it could be written SALLY = PITCHER, just as it was written X = 1.

Then SALLY could be changed to catcher, or SALLY = CATCHER. Perhaps the team rotates, so SALLY will be playing many different positions. So SALLY = FIRST BASE, SALLY = SHORTSTOP, and so on. The coach might write "NEXT SALLY" to remind him when it's time to change her to the next position.

X = 1: NEXT X	SALLY = PITCHER: NEXT SALLY
X = 2: NEXT X	SALLY = CATCHER: NEXT SALLY
X = 3: NEXT X	SALLY = FIRST BASE: NEXT SALLY
X = 4: NEXT X	SALLY = SECOND BASE: NEXT SALLY
X = 5: NEXT X	SALLY = THIRD BASE: NEXT SALLY

In a program, this would be written FOR X = 1 TO 5: NEXT X.

O.K. SALLY, RIGHT OVER THE PLATE.

FOR-NEXT can be used in more ways than just for a delay loop. FOR-NEXT is an important method to repeat any action. With a delay loop, the computer quietly counts inside the memory. The computer is asked to do nothing else but count to delay the next action. However, if a command is placed between FOR and NEXT, the computer will do that action the number of times requested.

Write a program that will write a sentence several times.

Here's an example for you to study and type:

```
NEW
10 HOME
20 FOR X = 1 TO 10
30 PRINT "I CAN WRITE THIS 10 TIMES?"
40 NEXT X
50 END
```

RUN the program.

Now the computer will not only count, it will print what is in LINE 30 as it counts. This type of action is one of the greatest benefits of using a computer. Something may be repeated endless times much faster than any human ever could!

If only computers could do dishes! With robots becoming more of a possible addition to every household, even dishwashing probably will soon be done by computers. Even when using a dishwasher, a human still has to do too much repetitious work to rinse, stack, unload, etc. It is the same action over and over with each dish until the job is finished. Only humans dislike monotonous repetition. Computers don't have emotions, so they don't mind one "bit" repeating monotonous actions!

Variables can change what they represent.

Variables play an essential role when using computers; they help make repetitions possible because they can change in what they represent. Think some more about Sally being able to have more than one position on the team, and X or any other letter being able to represent more than one amount, until it starts to make sense to you. Sally can represent many positions on a team, and X can represent many different amounts.

Now to get off the baseball field and back to computer business! It is usually easier to use an actual word as a variable to represent an amount. For example:

LUNCH = 5 is very understandable, right? No? Think about it again! Here's how a report of the cost of lunches for one week could be written, using the variable LUNCH to represent the price of each lunch:

LUNCH = 3
LUNCH = 2
LUNCH = 6
LUNCH = 4
LUNCH = 5
LUNCHES = 20

So the variable LUNCH actually represents five different amounts. "Make friends" with variables. They really are not so strange, after all. Variables are used in algebra all the time. By the way, algebra isn't really all that difficult if you learn it step by step, just as you are learning to use a computer.

Variables are used in figuring math.

Variables can be used for more than with FOR-NEXT loops. They are used a great deal when figuring math. Sometimes LET is used with variables, but with an Apple computer, it is not necessary. If you want to use LET to help you remember that you are "letting" a variable equal an amount, go ahead. It won't affect your program. The expression LET X = 2 indicates the computer is letting X represent, or take the place of, 2. It is quicker to say X = 2. On an Apple, it means the same thing. Study and type the following:

Input	**Process**
NEW	(Clears memory)
10 HOME	(Clears screen)
20 X = 3	(Assigns a value to the variable)
30 PRINT X	(Prints the value of X on screen)
40 END	(Terminates or ends the program)

What will be on the screen when this program is run? You are absolutely correct . . . 3 is the answer!

Now type another program using two variables. Use different letters if more than one variable is used within the same program.

Input	Process
NEW	(Clears memory)
10 HOME	(Clears screen)
20 X = 10	(Assigns a value to X)
30 Y = 30	(Assigns a value to Y)
40 PRINT Y − X	(Subtracts the value of X from Y and prints it on the screen)
50 END	(Terminates or ends the program)

Now what will be on the screen when the program is executed? RUN it to see if you were correct.

(Did you get 20 before the computer told you?)

String variables are used to represent alphabetic letters and symbols.

The computer is made so that it understands numbers, but it needs help to read alphabetic letters or symbols. When a variable is going to represent anything that is not a number, it must be changed to a **string variable**. The dollar sign ($) is the symbol used to represent a string. It always comes after the letter or letters used; the computer handles the characters as if they were a string of characters strung together.

String variables can represent either numbers, symbols, or letters of the alphabet; however, plain variables are usually used to represent numbers.

Literals placed within quotes are used with string variables. For example, A$ = "SALLY."

The quotes are necessary to mark off how many letters belong to the string of characters the STRING VARIABLE represents.

Type and study the following:

NEW	(Clears memory)
10 HOME	(Clears the screen)
20 NAME$ = "SALLY"	(Assigns a value to the string variable)
30 PRINT NAME$	(Prints the value assigned)
40 END	(Terminates)

Notice when you RUN the program, SALLY is printed, not NAME$. NAME$ has been assigned to represent the word "SALLY." So when the computer is told to print NAME$, SALLY is printed instead.

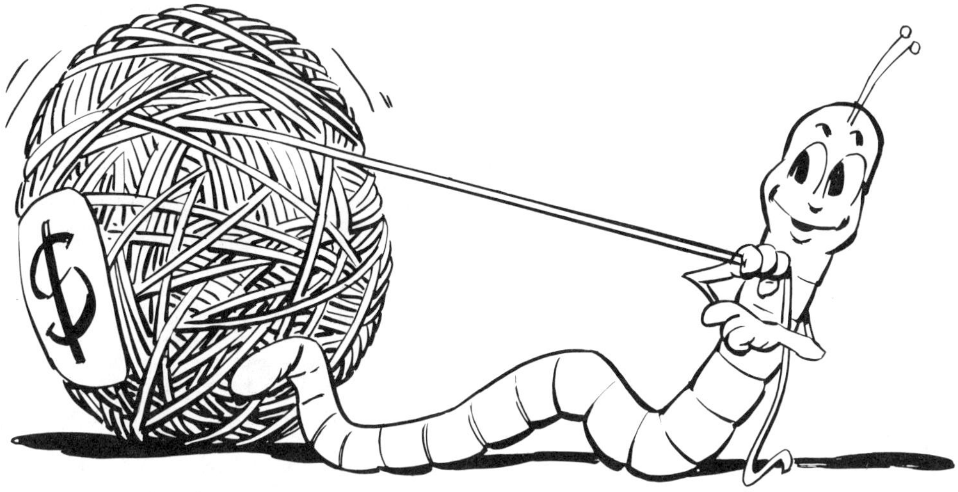

THE $ REPRESENTS THE END OF A STRING OF CHARACTERS.

String variables are used in notes and letters.

By using **string variables**, you can write a short note on the screen that says the same thing to many different people, by just changing what the string variable is to represent.

Study and type the following program:

```
NEW
10 HOME
15 REM WRITE A NOTE USING STRING VARIABLES
20 VTAB 5
25 NAME$ = "LISA"
30 PRINT "DEAR  ";NAME$ (Leave a space
                        before the last
                        quote to leave a
                        space between
                        printed words.)
50 ?:?
60 PRINT "PLEASE BUY SOME MILK AND BREAD."
70 ?:?:?
80 PRINT "LOVE"
90 PRINT "MOM"
100 END
```

RUN the program to see the "computer style note"! Now LIST the program and type Line 25 again to change the name.

```
25 NAME$ = "DEAN"
```

Now RUN the program.

Notice the last name assigned to the **string variable** NAME$ replaces the former name, so DEAN replaced LISA when Line 25 was changed. Now, you add a new name and see it change again.

Learn to save programs on a disk.

Now that you are beginning to write longer programs, you should start saving programs on a disk. When you turn off the computer, it erases memory which wipes out all your hard work. With your program saved on a disk, you can boot up the disk and begin typing right where you left off. Anything that saves retyping and hours of work must be good! Right?

Here's how you save on a disk:

1. Be certain the disk operating system has been booted before you start typing. It's a good idea to always have a booted disk ready to store information every time you enter data from the keyboard. The disk in the disk drive must already have been initialized and be ready to receive information. Make sure the disk you use has a write-enable notch.

   (Check back to Chapter 3 if you need to review these "pesky" details! It might save you time.)
2. Type a program and give it a name. Use a name from a REM to make it easier to remember. Keep the name of the program short and simple.
3. Type SAVE followed by the name of the program in capital letters. If you have more than one disk drive, you must indicate in which drive you wish to save. If you are using an Apple IIc, you can't have blank spaces between words. Place periods between words
   Example: MY.PROGRAM
   SAVE MY.PROGRAM,D1 (using the first disk drive)
   SAVE MY.PROGRAM,D2 (using the second disk drive)

After you type SAVE and press [RETURN], the disk drive will light up, and you'll hear the disk drive busily bringing your program from RAM and saving it on the disk.

Now type CATALOG to see if your program is listed in the directory. If for some reason your program didn't get saved on the disk, repeat the entire procedure. Check your disk if an I/O ERROR appears on the screen.

The LOAD command sends information from the disk to RAM.

LOAD is a command that sends the data that has been saved on a disk to RAM memory where it is stored temporarily. The original data is still stored on the disk. There are two copies of the data now—one on the disk and one in RAM.

If you have a long program to type, you can save part of the program on a disk. You can complete the entire program later. Just boot the disk on which the program is saved, type the rest of the program and save the revised, completed program on the disk. Without the advantage of saving on a disk, you have to start all over again every time you want to type a long program that can't be finished in a short time.

After typing LOAD (NAME OF PROGRAM), you will notice the red light on the drive light up. When it goes off, you must type LIST to see your program listing or type RUN to see the output from the program. Nothing appears on the screen if you type just the LOAD command. The RUN (NAME OF PROGRAM) can also be used to bring a program from the disk into memory. With this command, the program output is seen on the screen. Errors in the program will be reported if this command is used. If the program is not completed, several errors may be reported because all the lines have not been completed. This is one disadvantage of using RUN to start your incomplete programs. It is best to just use LOAD and LIST if you want to finish an incomplete program.

SAVE a program.

Practice saving this program so you'll know how to save your own programs. Insert an initialized disk, and here we go! Type the following:

```
NEW
10 HOME
15 REM FIRST NOTE
20 VTAB 5
30 NAME$ = "LISA"
40 PRINT "DEAR; "NAME$
50 ?:?
60 PRINT "PLEASE BUY MILK AND BREAD"
70 ?:?:?
80 PRINT "LOVE"
90 PRINT "MOM"
100 END
```

Now run the program to make certain it works. List the program, so you can make any necessary corrections before you save your masterpiece.

Now type:

```
SAVE FIRST NOTE and press [RETURN].
```

(Remember to place a period between FIRST.NOTE if you are using an Apple IIc.)

You will hear the disk drive saving your program. After the disk drive has stopped, turn off the computer to wipe out your program from memory. Now turn the computer on again to boot your disk. Now load your program back from the disk where it was saved, into the computer memory by typing the following:

```
LOAD FIRST NOTE and press [RETURN].
```

Type LIST to the program listing or RUN to see the output.

Learn more about variables and string variables.

Variables and **string variables** may be used together in writing letters. Study and type the following:

Input **Explanation**

```
NEW
5 REM A SHORT LETTER                (Documents the title)
10 HOME
20 VTAB 6                           (Spaces down six from top)
30 D$ = "MARCH 1"                   (Assigns a value to D$ for the date)
35 PRINT D$                         (Prints the date)
40 PRINT:PRINT:PRINT                (Leaves three blank lines)

50 NAME$ = "JENNY"                  (Assigns a value to NAME$)
60 PRINT "DEAR "; NAME$             (Prints Dear Jenny)

70 PRINT
80 PRINT "THANKS FOR THE LOAN."
90 M$ = "$4"                        (Assigns a value to M$ for money)

100 PRINT "THE ";M$
110 PRINT "REALLY CAME IN HANDY"

115 ?                               (Leaves one blank line)
120 PRINT "THANKS VERY MUCH."       (Prints literal)
130 ?                               (Leaves one blank line)

140 S$ = "JOE"                      (Assigns value to S$ for sender)
150 PRINT "LOVE"                    (Prints literal)

160 ?:?:?                           (Leaves three blank lines)
170 PRINT S$                        (Prints Joe)

180 END                             (Sets terminal)
```

Run the program to see this letter.

Now change the program by changing the date, names, and amount of money mentioned in the letter. Change lines 30, 50, 90, and 140. For example:

```
30 D$ = "JULY 1"
50 NAME$ = "CAROL"
90 M$ = "$10"
140 S$ = "RICH"
```

Draw a picture on your screen.

It is possible to draw pictures on your screen by arranging characters in various shapes to represent people or things. For example, here are two pictures. Can you tell what they are supposed to be?

```
                             v
                            vvv
aaaaaaaaaaaaaaa           vvvvvvv
a             a         vvvvvvvvvv
a   v    v    a        vvvvvvvvvvvvv
a             a      vvvvvvvvvvvvvvvvvv
a      v      a   vvvvvvvvvvvvvvvvvvvvvvv
a             a  vvvvvvvvvvvvvvvvvvvvvvvvvv
a      0      a              -
                           -----
```

Try drawing on your screen. Let your imagination be your guide. It's fun to be creative. The computer can really be great fun once you feel more at home as you use it!

Use program design to improve your programs.

Programs should be planned and designed in advance before sitting down at a computer. **Screen spacing charts** are very necessary and helpful in designing the output on the monitor screen.

There are samples of a screen spacing chart on the following pages. Notice that the horizontal spacing from left side to right side goes from 1 to 40, making 40 spaces available. The vertical spacing goes from 1 to 24, making 24 spaces available.

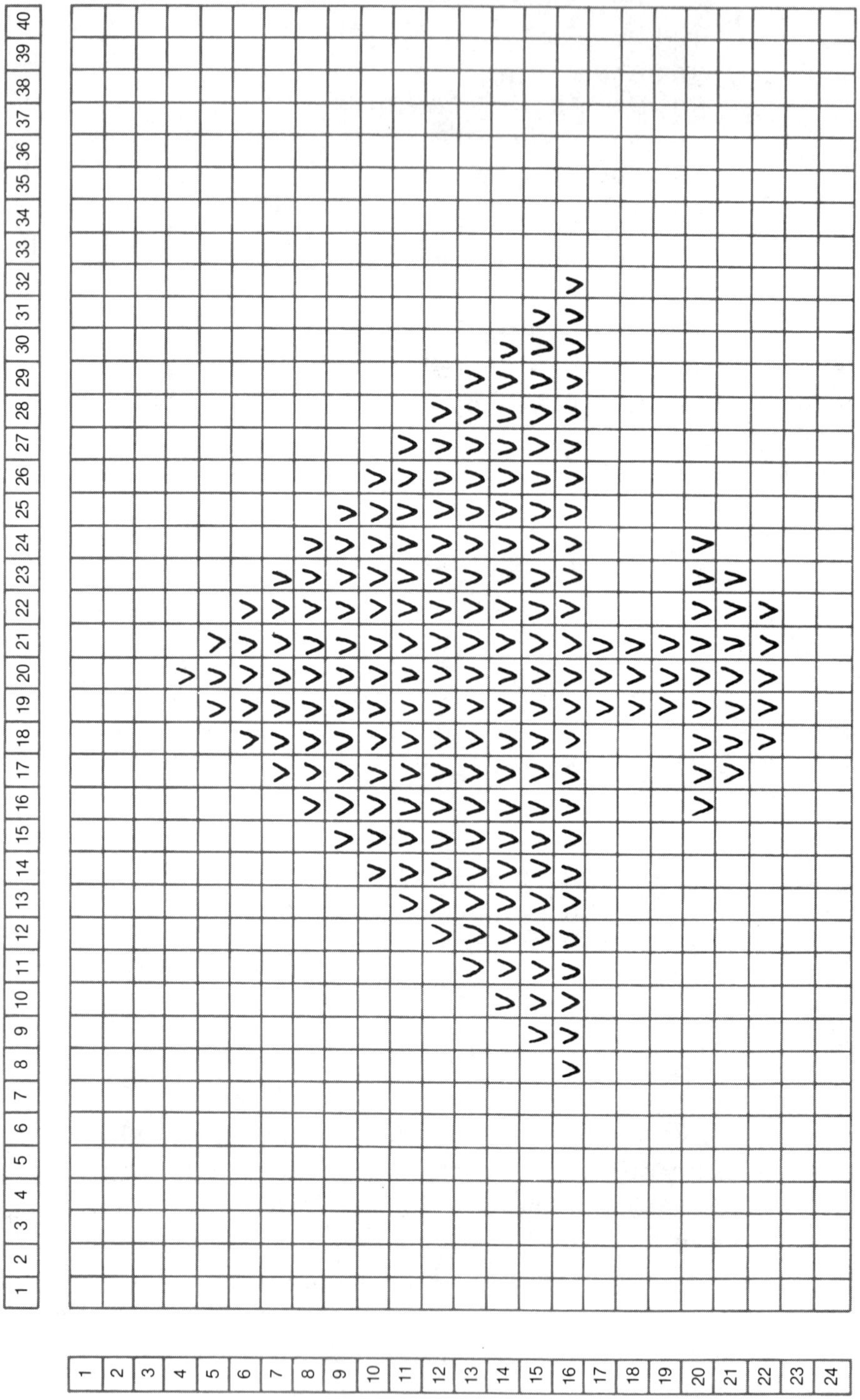

Use the chart to design a program that will draw a picture using characters from the keyboard. This is similar to what an architect does as he uses blueprints to design a house before actual construction takes place. Most things prove to be better if they are preplanned and organized.

A sample tree is drawn on the first screen chart to give you an idea of what to do. To type the tree, space down four lines from the top and over 20 spaces from the left. Then type a V or whatever character you wish. From there on, move down a line and add one more character each time you type a new line. You will be watching both the screen and chart to see what to do next. After you get the position to start from the chart, you will primarily be looking at the screen. It should be easier to do than it has been to describe. Have fun!

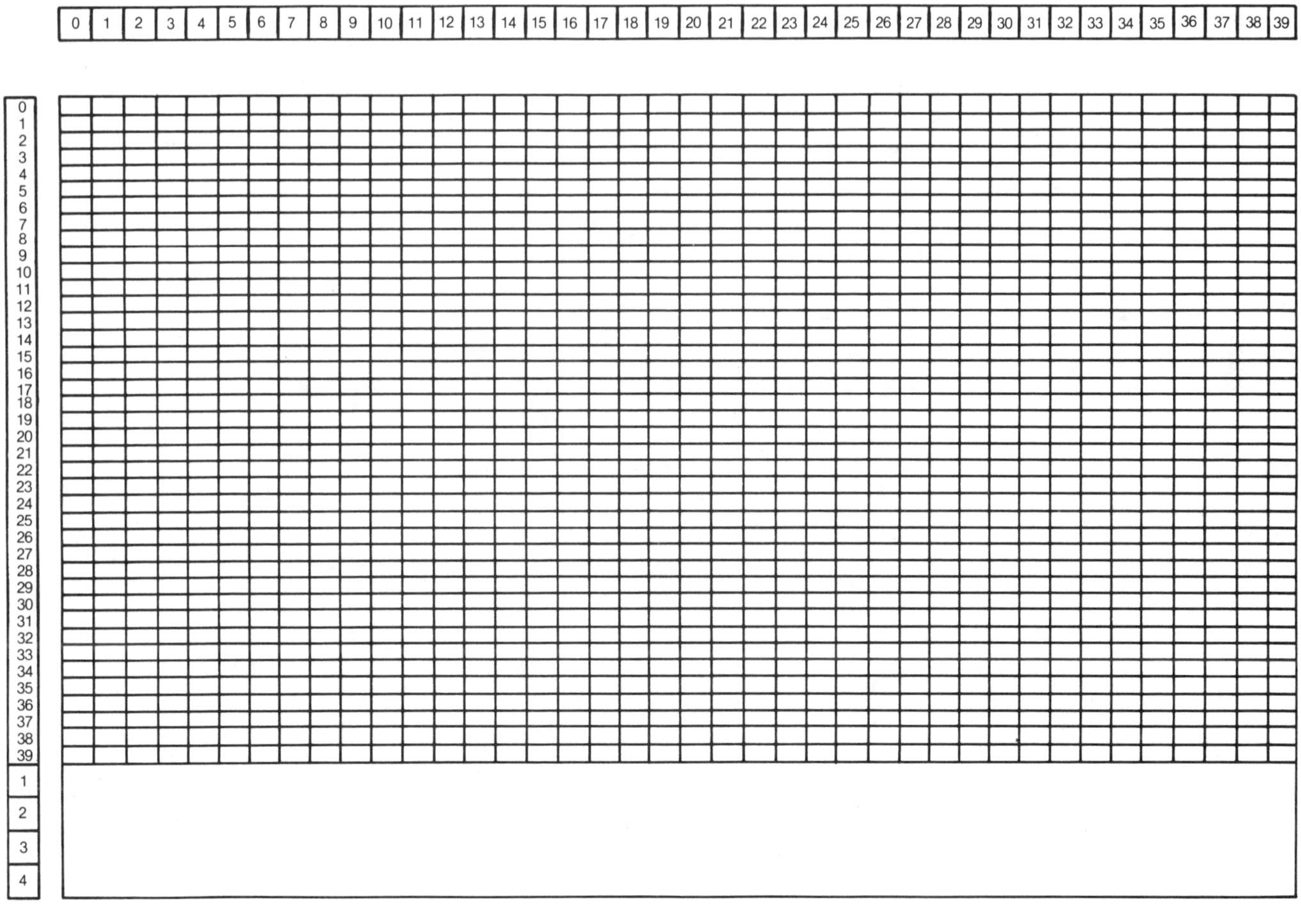

Use screen spacing charts for text.

Screen spacing charts can be used for regular messages, called text, as well as designs. The note you wrote earlier in this lesson can be designed on a text screen spacing chart. Study the next page where the short note has been arranged on a chart.

Notice that the first line, which is called a salutation, begins five lines down from the top, so a VTAB 5 command could be given to make the cursor move down to the right spot. Notice this same line starts over eleven spaces from the left margin; an HTAB 11 command would place it there. To leave some space between the salutation and the rest of the note, two blank lines are to be printed.

PRINT:PRINT would do the job nicely!

Next, the main message needs to be moved over eleven spaces in order to match the salutation. So another HTAB 11 is needed, followed by PRINT "PLEASE BUY MILK AND BREAD."

Now two more blank lines are needed. Use two more PRINT statements to do the job. The closing, which is called "a complimentary close," is spaced over nineteen spaces from the left margin; so another HTAB 19 is needed. Next, the PRINT "LOVE" comes, followed by two more blank lines, PRINT:PRINT. Another HTAB 19 is necessary to match the horizontal position of the complimentary close; then finally, the last PRINT "MOM" ends the message.

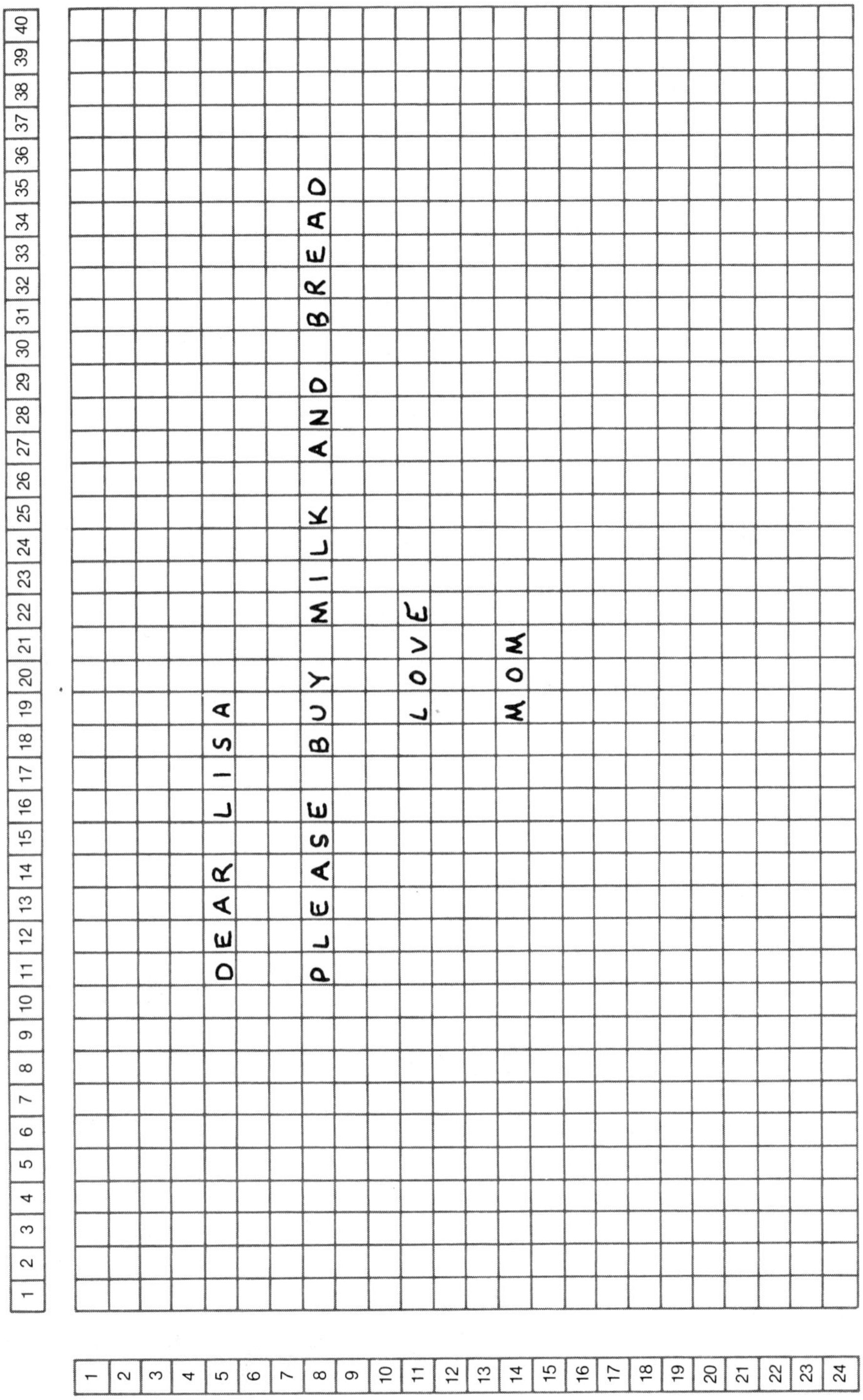
DEAR LISA
PLEASE BUY MILK AND BREAD
LOVE
MOM

Write a program using information from a screen spacing chart.

The program written on the **screen spacing chart** should be arranged so the computer can understand the instructions. The program has related lines grouped together for easier reading.

```
NEW
10 HOME
15 REM WRITE A NOTE WITH ATTRACTIVE SPACING
20 VTAB 5:HTAB 11: PRINT "DEAR LISA"
30 PRINT:PRINT
40 HTAB 11: PRINT "PLEASE BUY ";
45 PRINT "MILK AND BREAD."
50 PRINT:PRINT
60 HTAB 19:PRINT "LOVE"
70 PRINT:PRINT: HTAB 19: PRINT "MOM"
```

Remember, more than one command can be on one line if the commands are separated by colons (:).

Buy or make several charts so you can design other messages. It's fun to see how your output is going to look on paper before you waste time trying things out by trial and error at the computer. You will be able to make the computer put words and designs right where you have planned. Now you will start to feel more like the boss of the computer . . . and that's the way it's supposed to feel! Remember, you're the one with the magnificent mind!

VOCABULARY TO REMEMBER

BASIC Commands

REM Command used for documentation purposes to give information and explanations about a program. Stands for remark.

HTAB Command which can be used to center characters horizontally on the screen.

VTAB	Command which can be used to center characters vertically on the screen.
PRINT TAB	Command which moves the cursor to a specified position on the screen. Used to make columns.
INVERSE	Command which reverses the normal screen lighting so that characters are dark and the background is light.
FLASH	INVERSE command which gives flashing effect to characters on the screen.
NORMAL	Command which returns the screen to normal lighting, which is dark background with light letters.
FOR-NEXT	Statement which instructs the computer to repeat a task a specified number of times.
SPEED =	Command which regulates the speed at which program is listed or executed. The range is from 1 to 255.
SAVE	Command which saves programs on storage devices outside the main computer memory.
LOAD	Command which moves data from a computer storage device and stores it into RAM memory.

Terms

Document	To give information which helps to make a program more understandable.
String Variable	A symbol which can change what it represents. It can represent a group of alphabetic, numeric or alphanumeric characters which are stored together in memory.

Program Design Planning a program "on paper" to decide what the program is to do, and how it will appear as output.

Screen Spacing Chart Chart used to design program output.

CREATIVE CORNER

Now you are beginning to know how to handle your APPLE and can give it instructions to make it do some of the things you plan. You should be very proud of yourself!

Using what you've learned in Chapters 5 and 6, write some original programs.

1. Using the program below as a model, instruct the computer to print your name 5 times. Substitute your name for "SALLY" in line 30.

```
NEW
10 HOME
20 FOR X = 1 TO 5
30 PRINT "SALLY"
40 NEXT X
50 END
```

2. Write a program using REM, HTAB, VTAB, INVERSE, PRINT, and NORMAL that prints your favorite holidays.
3. Write a program using REM, HOME, PRINT, and FOR-NEXT that will print your name six times. Next, change the name and the number of times to 10. What lines need to be changed?
4. Write a short note that can be sent to several friends. (Use string variables, variables, VTAB, HTAB, and PRINT.)

Remember to check back in Chapters 5 and 6 if you need to review. Read each problem carefully to know what you are supposed to do; think of ways to solve the problem. Study similar problems in Chapters 5 and 6. Find the commands that will get the computer to do what you want; then write the program.

7
USING THE PRINTER WITH A COMPUTER

GOAL: To gain an understanding of printers.

THOUGHT: Your printed words represent you!

Vocabulary To Learn:

BASIC Commands: PR#1 PR#0

TERMS:

HARD COPY	IMPACT PRINTER	PLOTTER
PERIPHERAL	NON-IMPACT PRINTER	TRACTOR-FEED PRINTER
PRINTER INTERFACE CARD	THERMAL PRINTER	FRICTION-FEED PRINTER
SERIAL PRINTER	LETTER-QUALITY PRINTER	COUNTER
PARALLEL PRINTER	DOT MATRIX PRINTER	

Plan to use a printer with your computer.

It is very important to learn how to use a printer with a computer. Being able to print output on paper makes the work done on a computer much more lasting and valuable. Printed data which someone can handle and read is called **hard copy**.

All the output in earlier chapters has been on the monitor. In this chapter you will learn to send output to the printer. A printer is a **peripheral** device used with the computer to print data after it has been processed. If you don't have a printer, read this chapter to learn about the different types of printers and write the programs, leaving out the lines which activate the printer, lines which contain PR#1 and PR#0. Your programs will not run if you have PR#1 and/or PR#0 in your listings and don't have a printer connected to your computer.

Remember the commands INVERSE and FLASH do not work when you use the printer as output! These commands are used only when the monitor is the output device.

Printers can print very rapidly.

Printers are classified by speed and by the method and quality of printing. All computers print faster than humans can type; however, some printers are classified "low-speed." Low speed printers are frequently used with microcomputers, such as the Apple. Some "slow" printers can print up to 300 lines per minute, which is approximately 700 to 900 words per minute. The cost of a low-speed printer is approximately $500 and up.

High-speed printers and very-high-speed printers cost much more—from about $3,000 to more than $300,000. Some of the printers can print more than 20,000 lines per minute. These printers are able to print an entire line or even a whole page at one time.

The average personal computer user doesn't need an extremely fast, expensive printer; however, it is possible to connect the Apple with almost every type of printer available —expensive or inexpensive! Always check with an Apple dealer before purchasing any printer to make certain it will work with your Apple model.

PHEW! LOOK AT THAT PRINTER GO!

The printer must be connected to the computer.

An appropriate **printer interface card** and cable are necessary to join a printer to a computer. The printer interface card is placed in a slot located inside the computer, and the cable joins the printer to it. If you are using an Apple IIc, the printer plugs into the card through the portal for the printer at the back of the computer.

Printers are classified by the type of signals they receive.

Serial printers receive signals from the computer one bit at a time. Remember, it takes eight bits to make one byte or one character. **Parallel printers** receive information from the computers eight bits at a time. The Apple IIc is designed to work only with serial printers. You can't use a parallel printer with an Apple IIc.

Printers are classified by their method of printing.

Printers are classified as **impact** and **non-impact**. The **impact printer** prints by striking the paper, ribbon, and character at one time—similar to the action of a typewriter. The inked ribbon transfers the character onto the paper as it is pressed to the paper by the character key bar.

Some typewriters are designed to be used with computers; however, the keys on the typewriters jam because they cannot keep up with the speed of characters coming from the computer. Manual typewriters are not being made any more. Even electric and electronic typewriters may soon be considered to be old-fashioned equipment because of the rapidly expanding printer and computer technology.

Printers are classified impact or non-impact.

Non-impact printers use heat, photography, or jet ink-spray methods to print.

Special paper is usually necessary when using a non-impact printer, such as a thermal printer. The paper must be treated or coated so it will respond to heat.

Non-impact printers are much quieter and faster than impact printers; however, it is not possible to make copies on a non-impact printer. Thermal printers have not been very popular in the past; documents produced on the special thermal paper turned yellow as they aged and could not be left in the sun or exposed to heat.

HERE'S AN EXAMPLE OF IMPACT AND NON-IMPACT PRINTING.

The Apple Scribe printer is an example of improved printer technology.

The Apple Scribe printer is an impact printer that uses a thermal process. A special ribbon is heated and pressed against normal paper by the printing hammers to produce an image. Regular paper can be used with this printer so the aging and yellowing of thermal paper have been eliminated. The special ribbon comes with four colors so the printer can print text and pictures in color.

Dot matrix printers are impact printers.

Printing on an impact printer is of either letter or dot matrix quality. With dot matrix, the character is made up of a series of tiny dots. In the past, the quality of printing of a solid-letter printer was much better than the quality of a **dot matrix printer**. The dots distorted the characters, making some hard copy difficult to read. Solid-letter printers were called "letter-quality," meaning, of course, that the printing was attractive enough to be used for letters.

The quality of the output of new dot matrix printers has been greatly improved; the dots printed by the later models are so small and close together that it is difficult to see the dots without using a magnifying glass. The characters are not distorted, and the printing is attractive enough to be used for correspondence, such as letters to customers, etc.

Dot matrix printers are versatile.

Even though they are less expensive than letter-quality printers, dot matrix printers can produce a greater variety of printing. Letter-quality printers are limited in the types of printing they can produce; however, they do produce a higher quality print than even a fine electric typewriter and can use ordinary paper. The Apple Daisy-Wheel which is a letter-quality printer costs about $2,000.

Dot matrix printers can print a variety of sizes, thicknesses, and styles of printing. Dot matrix printers can also be used to print pictures and graphics.

The Apple Imagewriter is an excellent dot matrix printer that can be used with all Apple models if certain adjustments are made. The Imagewriter is very fast and produces high quality print in a variety of sizes and styles.

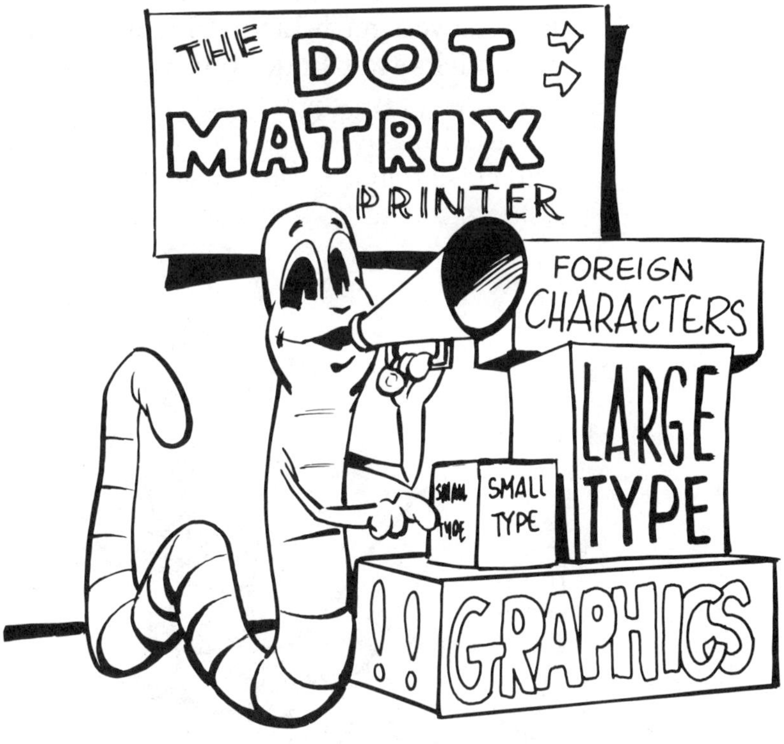

COME SEE WHAT A DOT MATRIX PRINTER CAN DO!

A Plotter is a specially designed printer to print graphics.

The Apple Color Plotter can reproduce graphs, charts, floor plans, and other pictures or graphics you might want to create with your computer. It must be used with graphics software.

Technological improvements in printers are rapidly being made. Try to find out the latest developments before purchasing a printer that might be out of date. Remember, always get the most you can for your money.

Printer manuals can be difficult to understand.

Try to buy a printer that has an understandable manual of instructions that comes with it. Printer manufacturers design printers that can be used with all makes and models of computers; therefore, the instructions in the manuals are usually very technical and don't give specific instructions for installing or operating the printer with a specific kind of computer. Even someone who isn't a beginner must study diligently to try to understand the jargon of the printer manuals. Don't become frustrated if you must read and reread printer instructions to know what to do. You are not alone. All but the most expert computer operators must ponder over a new printer manual, trying to make it apply to a specific computer.

It might be advisable to ask your salesman to adjust a new printer before you leave the store to make certain it will work with your computer. Then, you can start using your printer as soon as you get it home to learn some of the printing applications and tricks that make having a printer so great.

SOMETIMES IT'S DIFFICULT TO UNDERSTAND A PRINTER MANUAL.

Paper with pin-feed holes is used for printers.

Paper for printers comes with holes on both side margins so that it can be attached to the pin feed area on the printer. The paper is carefully inserted so that the holes on each side have a pin from the printer to guide them up into place. It is better to have tractor feeds that are adjustable, so that paper of various widths can be inserted and printed. This will allow for labels and small cards to be printed. Friction feed is available on some printers, so paper without pin holes such as stationery and envelopes may be printed.

Most **tractor-feed printer** paper is made so that it continuously feeds into the printer. After printing, each page can be separated easily from the preceding page along the perforated edge.

Paper comes in different qualities and styles. Less expensive, lined paper is used for reports such as accounting; plain paper is used for correspondence and formal manuscripts.

I DON'T THINK THIS IS WHAT THE AUTHOR MEANT WHEN SHE DESCRIBED "TRACTOR FEED."

Turn on the printer by typing PR#1.

The printer is attached to a **printer interface card** which is usually placed in Slot #1 inside the computer. All commands are directed to Slot #1 to communicate with the computer. Remember the disk drive is usually put into Slot #6. This is why the disk drive is started by typing PR#6.

As you type PR#1, the card leading to the printer is turned on and becomes ready to receive orders. Make sure your printer is plugged in and has all the necessary switches in the on positions.

Now type the following:

```
NEW
10 HOME
20 PRINT "HI PRINTER . . . ARE YOU WORKING?"
```

Now type PR#1 and press [RETURN].

Now type LIST. On some Apples the word "LIST" won't show on the screen; the computer acts as if it's waiting for you to press [RETURN]. After you press [RETURN], your listed program should print out as hard copy on your printer.

"PR#1" TURNS IT ON.

Type PR#0 to turn off the printer.

To take the control away from the **printer interface card**, type PR#0. Now things are back as they were before you used the printer.

It is a big advantage to print out your program listings. You will be able to see the entire program listings when you want to update and change your program. It is also easier to check for mistakes in spelling, English, and punctuation.

You will be able to print out your program by typing the command PR#1 as part of the program. See Line 20. Study and type the following:

Input **Process**

```
NEW
10 HOME
20 PR#1                             (Slot #1 turned on)
30 PRINT "TO PRINT THIS"            (Prints on printer)
40 PR#0                             (Slot #1 turned off)
50 VTAB 8:HTAB 10                   (Vertically and horizontally)
60 PRINT "BUT NOT THIS ONE"         (Prints on screen only)
70 VTAB 12:HTAB 8                   (Vertically and horizontally)
80 PRINT "PR#1 and PR#0 ";
85  PRINT "CONTROL PRINTER OUTPUT"
```

CONTROL PASSES BACK AND FORTH BETWEEN THE PRINTER AND THE COMPUTER.

Type RUN and see the message first on your printer, then on your screen only. (Take out Line 20.) Type LIST to see your program on the screen. Next, type PR#1 and type LIST to see it on your printer. Don't forget to press [RETURN] after each command.

Print a program in immediate execution.

Now type some of the programs from earlier chapters and use the printer for output. Using immediate execution, the printer can print this program after you type the following:

```
NEW
PR#1
PRINT "LIFE IS A GREAT ADVENTURE."
```

(The printer will print the sentence twice, just as it would on the screen in immediate execution.)

Print a program in delayed execution.

Now use line numbers to print the program in delayed execution.

```
NEW
10 HOME
20 PRINT "NIBBLES IS TEACHING ME."
30 PRINT "I LIKE NIBBLES!"
40 END
```

Type PR#1.
Press [RETURN].
Type LIST and press [RETURN] and see your program listed on the printer.

Use a line number with PR#1 to print hard copy.

Now type a program to print the output of the program, not just the program listing. To do this, the PR#1 must be written with a line number in the program. Type the following:

Input	Process
`NEW`	
`5 HOME`	
`10 PR#1`	(Turns control to the PRINTER INTERFACE CARD.)
`20 PRINT "THE COMPUTER READS ";`	
`25 PRINT "LINES CORRECTLY"`	
`30 PRINT "EVEN WHEN YOU PUT NUMBERS"`	
`40 PRINT "IN THE"`	
`50 PRINT "WRONG ORDER."`	
`60 PR#0`	(Returns control to computer.)
`70 END`	

To make printed output more attractive, it can be arranged vertically and horizontally. Most printers have 80 spaces horizontally, making 40 the center of the paper. The center of the regular monitor screen is 20 because the screen has 40 spaces horizontally. It is possible, however, to have 80 spaces on the screen if an 80-column card is inserted in a slot inside the computer. Then 40 would be the center point for both the monitor and the printer. The 80-column card is usually inserted in slot #3 in the Apple II or Apple II PLUS. There is a special auxiliary slot for this card in the Apple IIe. There is a switch above the keyboard on an Apple IIc that can be set to display 40 or 80 columns on the screen.

Use HTAB and PRINT statements to arrange hard copy.

Change the program on the preceding page by adding horizontal and vertical spacing commands. Remember, the horizontal center on the printer is 40 and the center of your screen is 20. This program might look strange on your screen without an 80-column card, but it should look attractive on the printed hard copy.

Study and type the following program:

```
Input                                   Process

NEW
10 HOME
20 PR#1                                 (Control to printer card)
30 HTAB 22                              (Moves to right 22 spaces)
40 PRINT "THE COMPUTER READS";
45 PRINT "LINES CORRECTLY"
50 PRINT:PRINT:PRINT                    (Makes three blank lines)
60 HTAB 29                              (Moves to right 29 spaces)
70 PRINT "EVEN WHEN YOU";
75 PRINT "PUT NUMBERS"
80 PRINT: PRINT: PRINT                  (Makes three blank lines)
90 HTAB 37                              (Moves to right 37 spaces)
100 PRINT "IN THE"
120 PRINT: PRINT: PRINT                 (Makes three blank lines)
130 HTAB 34                             (Moves to right 34 spaces)
140 PRINT "WRONG ORDER"
150 PR#0                                (Takes control away from card)
160 END                                 (Terminates program)
```

Now type RUN and press [RETURN] to see the program.

Print something several times using a GOTO loop.

Do you remember the program in Chapter 5 that repeated a sentence several times? Shhh . . . I'm going to give you a way to print it out as hard copy.

Do you remember the GOTO command? This command makes a line repeat endlessly. You can use this command to print something several times.

Study and type the following:

```
Input                                   Process

NEW
10 HOME
20 PR#1                                 (Sends control to the printer.)
30 PRINT "I WILL BE ";
35 PRINT "POLITE TO EVERYONE!"
40 GOTO 30                              (The computer is told to go back
                                        and write line 30 again.)
```

After you have typed the program, type RUN and press [RETURN]. You may run out of paper if you don't press [CONTROL] [C] or [CONTROL] [S] to stop the computer and printer! Isn't it easy to write something on paper over and over!

After you have stopped the runaway horse—that's the way a GOTO acts when it's left to itself—type PR#0 to change the control back from the printer interface card in Slot #1.

THIS IS EASY WITH A PRINTER.

Counters limit the number of loops made by GOTO.

A **counter** is a variable used with GOTO statements to place a limit on the number of times the computer will return to print a line.

The IF THEN command may be used in a program with a Counter and a GOTO. The computer is told IF the action or work is finished, THEN the computer should GOTO another line in the program. Here are some examples for you to study and type, using the printer as output:

Input	**Process**
NEW	
10 HOME	(Screen is cleared)
20 PR#1	(Control to Printer)
30 C = 0	(The variable C is "set" at 0)
40 PRINT "I WILL BE POLITE."	
50 C = C + 1	(Each time the sentence is printed, C has one added to the amount it was assigned, so now C = 0 + 1 which is the same as C = 1. One sentence has been printed)

```
60 IF C = 20 THEN GOTO 80        (If C = 20, the sentence has
                                  been printed 20 times; the
                                  computer goes to Line 80,
                                  skipping Line 70)

70 GOTO 40                       (Because C doesn't equal 20
                                  yet, the sentence hasn't been
                                  printed 20 times. The computer
                                  is told to GOTO Line 40 and
                                  print the sentence again)

80 PR#0                          (The control is taken from the
                                  printer interface card)

90 END                           (That's all folks!)
```

Type RUN and press [RETURN].

Now you won't have the computer acting like a runaway horse! The computer will stop printing after 20 lines.

Use a counter to limit the number of sentences to be printed.

If you want to change the number of times you will write the sentence "I WILL BE POLITE," or any other sentence you want to write in Line 40, just change Line 60.

60 IF C = 5 THEN GOTO 80. (This will make the sentence in this program print five times.)

Any value that you want to be compared with the variable C in Line 60 will be the number of times the sentence will print. If C = 2, the sentence will print two times. IF C = 4, the sentence will print four times. Don't change Line 30; C will still be given the value of 0 to begin.

Experiment with the program on the preceding page. Can you print "I WILL BE POLITE" 10 times? Or 3 times? Or 11 times?

What will you change? That's right . . . just change the value to be compared with the variable C in the IF statement in Line 60. That makes all the difference!

Now change the sentence on Line 40 so it prints new words; print the new sentence 10 times.

MY COMPUTER HELPS ME WRITE "I WILL BE POLITE" ANY NUMBER OF TIMES.

Print invitations to a party!

Here's a program that will let you send invitations or messages to your friends. Study and type the following program:

```
NEW
10 HOME

20 PR#1
30 VTAB 18
40 HTAB 20

50 PRINT "DEAR FRIEND"
60 PRINT:PRINT

70 HTAB 20
80 PRINT "COME TO MY PARTY ON SATURDAY,
   DEC. 1."
90 PRINT

100 HTAB 20
110 PRINT "IT WILL BE AT 3 P.M. AT MY
    HOME."

120 PRINT
130 HTAB 40
140 PRINT "LOVE"

150 PR#0
160 END
```

Run the program.

Change some of the sentences so that this program prints invitations to a special party you are going to have. Run the program as many times as you wish to print out invitations. Use each friend's name instead of "DEAR FRIEND" in Line 50. This will make them feel more special.

After the invitations have been printed, sign your name under LOVE. This will give your invitations a personal touch!

INVITATIONS ARE EASY WITH A PRINTER.

Use a FOR-NEXT loop to print several invitations.

To print the same invitation to several friends, use a FOR-NEXT loop. Add the following lines to the program on on the preceding page.

```
35 FOR X = 1 TO 3
                    (This will type three copies;
                    if you want to print more than three
                    copies, type the number of copies you
                    need. FOR X = 1 TO 5 would tell the
                    computer to print five copies;
                    FOR X = 1 TO 10 would print 10.
                    It's the last number in the equation
```

```
                     written after the word TO that
                     determines the number of times
                     something is to be repeated.)
142 PRINT:PRINT:PRINT:PRINT
                     (This will give spaces between the
                     notes.)
145 NEXT X
                     (This command sends the computer
                     back to line 30 in a loop.
                     The computer will continue to loop
                     until it reaches the number stated
                     after TO in the FOR-NEXT statement.)
```

Print a short note to a friend.

Here is another short note to be printed on the printer:

```
NEW

10 HOME
20 PR#1

30 PRINT:PRINT
40 HTAB 20
50 PRINT"DEAR SALLY"

60 PRINT:PRINT
70 HTAB 20
80 PRINT "I REALLY ENJOY MY APPLE . . .
   COMPUTER, THAT IS."

90 PRINT
100 HTAB 20
110 PRINT "LEARN TO USE AN APPLE WITH ME!"

120 HTAB 20
130  PRINT "NIBBLES WILL HELP US BOTH."

140 PRINT
150 HTAB 20
160 PRINT "LOVE"

170 PR#0
180 END
```

Type RUN and press [RETURN].

After you have seen this program work, change it so it will be up to date and match your life style.

Print a list of your friends' names and addresses.

Here is a program that will print names and phone numbers. It's always handy to have a list of your friends and their numbers. Change the name and number in Line 40, Line 60, and Line 80 to names and numbers of people you know. Remember, commas are used to make columns—if the words in the columns are not too long.

Study and type the following.

```
NEW
10 HOME
20 PR#1

30 HTAB 5
40 PRINT "SALLY", "944-5553"

50 HTAB 5
60 PRINT "JOE", "923-5577"

70 HTAB 5
80 PRINT "MARY", "834-4321"

90 PR #0
100 END
```

Type RUN and press [RETURN] and there's your list! Make the list as long as you wish by adding new lines with names and numbers, using the same commands in this program. I know you have lots of friends to call!

Use PRINT TAB to make columns.

If your friends have long names, use the PRINT TAB command to print the names in columns. (Commas allow for only short literals less than 14 characters in length.)

Study and type the following:

```
NEW
10 HOME
20 PR#1
25 PRINT:PRINT:PRINT
30 PRINT TAB (5); "SALLY ANN JOHNSON"; TAB
   (20); "934-4444"
40 PRINT
50 PRINT TAB (5); "PETER ALAN
   SMITHSON";TAB (20); "934-5555"

60 PR#0
70 END
```

Type RUN and press [RETURN].

The PRINT TAB(5) moves the sentence five spaces to the right —or whatever number of spaces is listed within the parentheses.

The semicolons (;) which follow the numbers in parentheses after PRINT TAB or TAB, and the semicolons which follow the literals —the names and numbers—instruct the computer to stay on the same line. The TAB instructs the computer to move over the number of spaces within the parentheses. Notice that only one PRINT statement is needed for the first PRINT TAB on a line. (The PRINT command affects all of the following TAB commands on the same line.)

The names or numbers within quotes are the literals which are to be printed.

Follow software directions for using printers.

When using the printer with professional disks, special instructions are usually necessary. Most commercial software requires some form of the PRINT command to produce hard copy. With APPLEWRITER, which is a program written for Apple IIe and Apple IIc, the command [CONTROL] [P] is used, followed by [N] [P], which indicates a new print.

Check the manual or instructions for the software you are using to learn how to use the printer with that particular program.

To print from your own programs which have been saved on disks, you may first have to type in a special command on some Apple II computers. This command is D$ = CHRS$(4) and is called D String, Character String 4. Then you type PRINT D$; "PR #1" to activate the printer. The DOS (Disk Operating System) is signaled that you are using a DOS command from within a BASIC program. Study your APPLE manual to learn more about this function.

Here are the special commands to type to print your own programs from a disk:

```
10 D$ = CHRS$(4)
20 PRINT D$;"PR#1"
```

VOCABULARY TO REMEMBER

BASIC commands

PR#1	Command which turns on the printer interface card in slot #1.
PR#0	Command which turns off the printer card.

Terms

Hard Copy	Information printed on paper and other items that can be read and held in the hand.
Peripheral	Device which can send and receive data from a computer, using interface cards and cables.
Printer Interface Card	Card which connects the cable between the computer and the printer.
Serial Printer	Printer that receives messages from the computer one bit at a time.
Parallel Printer	Printer that receives messages from the computer eight bits at a time.
Impact Printer	Device which prints by striking paper, ribbon and characters at the same time.
Non-Impact Printer	Printer that uses special paper that reacts to heat or other agents to produce written image.

Thermal Printer	Non-impact printer that uses heat and special paper to produce printed image.
Letter-Quality Printer	Printer which produces solid-print characters that are of consistent, high quality.
Dot Matrix Printer	Printer which produces characters which are formed by a series of small dots which may or may not be of good quality.
Plotter	Specially designed printer for graphics.
Tractor Feed Printer	Printer which can be adjusted to allow for various widths of tracter-feed paper to be printed.
Friction Feed Printer	Printer which allows regular paper without tractor-feed holes to be printed.
Counter	A variable used to count the number of repetitions in a loop.

CREATIVE CORNER

Once again, it's your turn to see how much you've learned as you studied this chapter.

Remember to check back in the chapter if you need to find an answer. That's how you can learn anything —by repeating something and using it until it becomes part of your memory and behavior! If you really know something, you can put that skill to work to make life easier and more fun.

Answer the following:

1. Into which slot in the computer is the printer interface card usually placed?
2. How can you determine whether printing is made with a dot matrix or a letter-quality printer?
3. How does an impact printer produce print?

4. Name the peripheral devices used with a computer.
5. What is hard copy?
6. What are the advantages of using a friction-feed printer? A tractor-feed printer?
7. What are the advantages and disadvantages of using a thermal printer?
8. What is the difference between an impact and non-impact printer?
9. What are the functions of the commands PR#1 and PR#0?

8
GRAPHICS

GOAL: To learn to draw using the Apple Computer.

THOUGHT: A picture can be worth a thousand words!

Aa Bb Cc Dd Ee Ff Gg Hh Ii Jj Kk Ll Mm

Vocabulary To Learn:

BASIC Commands:

GR	COLOR =	HGR2
HLIN	TEXT	HCOLOR
VLIN	STEP	HPLOT
PLOT	HGR	

TERMS:

GRAPHICS	TEXT WINDOW	CODE
LOW RESOLUTION GRAPHICS	HIGH RESOLUTION GRAPHICS	MOUSE
PIXELS		

Computers can be used to create drawings and charts.

Pictures, tables, and graphs are used by professional teachers, business executives, and lecturers to make learning and communicating more interesting and stimulating. Computer technology is making it easier to prepare these and other types of visual aids. Many new and exciting methods of producing **graphics** with a computer are being developed.

A PICTURE IS WORTH A THOUSAND WORDS.

Use the GR command for low resolution graphics.

One method of drawing with a computer is done by typing commands on the keyboard. The GR (graphics) command is used to make lines and dots (plots) appear on the monitor in **low resolution graphics**.

The screen is made up of horizontal and vertical grid lines, which form small boxes called **pixels**. (This stands for picture elements.) While in low resolution graphics mode, the screen has 40 spaces or grids horizontally, and 46 grids vertically.

The four lines at the bottom of the screen is called the **text window**. In the **graphics** mode, words or symbols can only be printed in the text window. The main area of the screen is reserved for lines or dots.

Study the screen spacing chart for graphics:

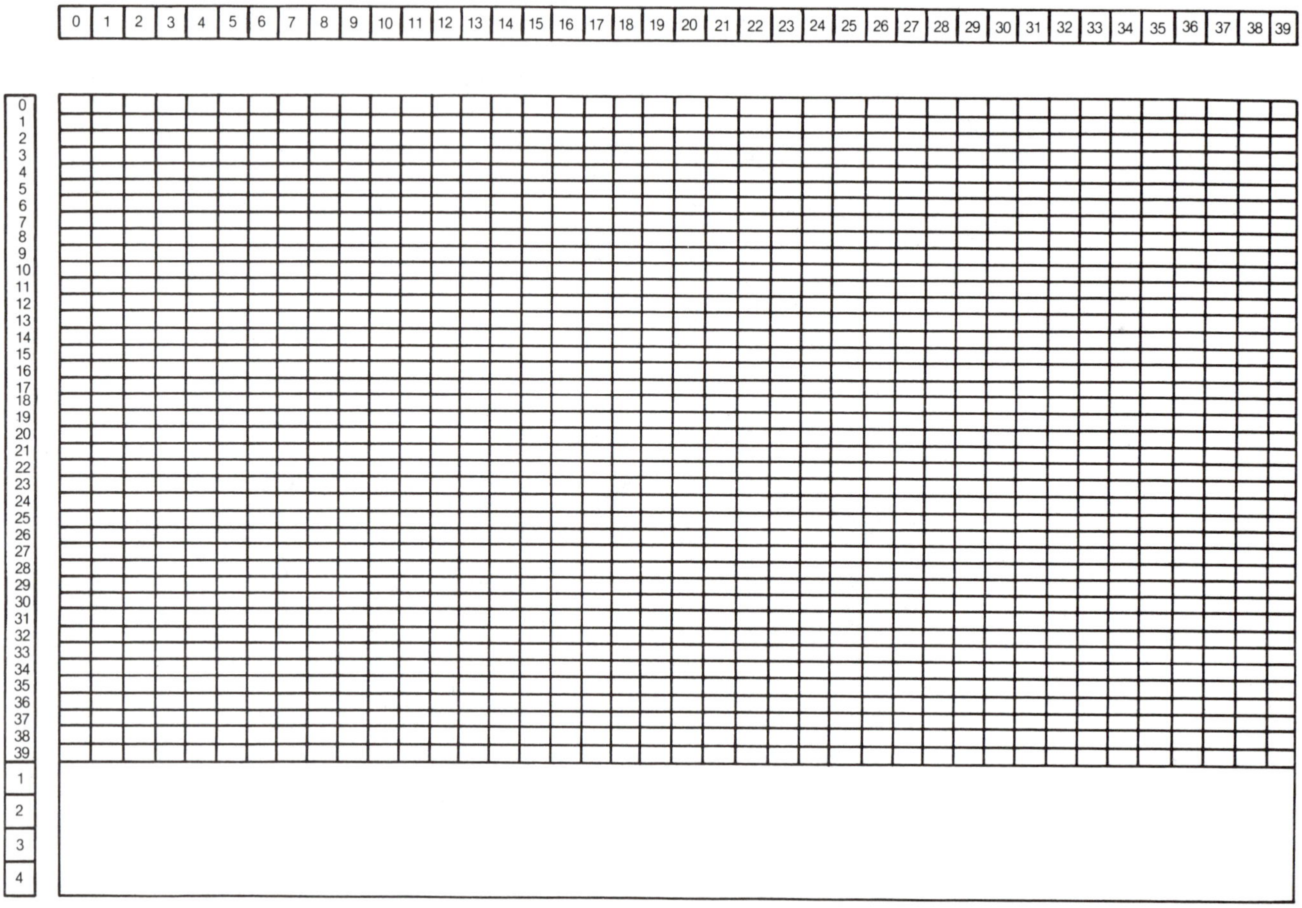

Use the HLIN and VLIN commands to draw lines.

The commands used for making horizontal and vertical lines in low resolution graphics are HLIN and VLIN. There are 40 spaces possible both horizontally and vertically on the monitor screen.

Study this example of an HLIN command:

Don't type these commands yet!

```
HLIN 1,39 AT 3
```

This command places a horizontal line across the screen from 1 to 39, located 3 lines down from the top.

Here is an example of a VLIN commmand:

```
VLIN 1, 39 AT 3
```

This command places a vertical line from 1 to 39, located 3 spaces over from the left margin.

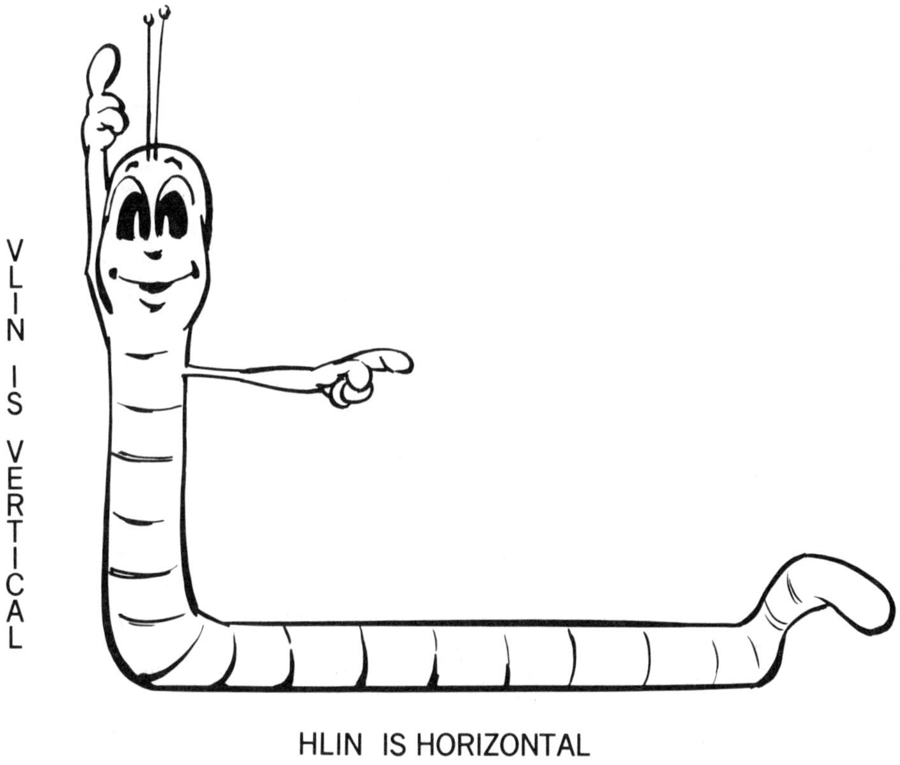

Draw dots on the screen using the PLOT command.

PLOT is the command used to draw points on the screen in low resolution graphics. The PLOT command is followed by numbers which give the horizontal and vertical location on the screen. The horizontal location always comes before the vertical.

Study this example of a PLOT command:

```
PLOT 3,5
```

This PLOT is three spaces over from the left margin horizontally, and five spaces down from the top vertically.

Study this example:

```
PLOT 20,38
```

This PLOT is located 20 spaces over from the left margin horizontally and 38 spaces down from the top vertically.

The horizontal location is frequently called the X axis; and the vertical, the Y axis.

Where would PLOT 4,8 be located?

(If you guessed four spaces over from the left margin and eight spaces down from the top, you were correct!)

This sounds more difficult than it actually is. As you begin to draw with your computer, this will make a lot more sense to you!

Write a graphics program.

Now let's put some of this new graphics knowledge to work and draw something on the screen. Are you ready? Good!

Type in the following program:

Input	Explanation
NEW HOME	(It's wise to always clear the memory and screen!)
10 HOME	(Clears the screen to get ready for the picture in this program.)
20 GR	(Sets graphics mode-to change from text (alphabet, numbers, etc.)
30 COLOR = 12	(Always use a color command with low resolution graphics. The higher the number, the lighter the shade.)
40 HLIN 0,39 AT 0	(This will be a horizontal line at the top of the screen.)

Type RUN and press [RETURN] to see this line. After you've seen the line, type TEXT and press [RETURN].

This will change graphics back into text mode which produces alphanumeric characters so you can continue typing your program. Notice that the word TEXT goes to the bottom of the screen, which is reserved for words.

You'll see "garbage" on your screen as the computer changes from graphics to text. Don't pay any attention to it.

Type HOME and press [RETURN]. Now type LIST and press [RETURN] and there's your program back again, so you can continue!

Always use the COLOR= command with low resolution graphics.

The COLOR= command must be used with GR graphics, even when using a black-and-white monitor. When no color command is given with low resolution graphics, the color comes up automatically in black. It cannot be seen because it is the same as the black background. (It's a good idea to put the color command on the same line with the GR command, so you won't forget to write it!)

This is an example of GR graphics command:

```
10 GR: COLOR = 4
```

There are 15 colors available in low resolution graphics. Numbers from 1 to 15 represent various colors.

0—BLACK	8—BROWN
1—MAGENTA (RED)	9—ORANGE
2—DARK BLUE	10—GREY
3—PURPLE	11—PINK
4—DARK GREEN	12—GREEN
5—GREY	13—YELLOW
6—MEDIUM BLUE	14—AQUA
7—LIGHT BLUE	15—WHITE

The colors will show only when viewed on a color monitor. On the regular non-color monitor, the colors will appear as various degrees of brightness. The darkest tones are given the lowest numbers. For example: zero (0) represents black. The higher the number, the lighter the color. The number 15 represents white.

Write a program using various colors.

Drawings are more interesting and varied if color is used; however, color is not available for text (alphabet, numbers, and symbols). Most people prefer a black-and-white monitor for programming using alphanumeric characters. The black-and-white monitor screen produces sharper text than a color monitor, making it easier to read.

If you have a monitor that produces color, the lines in the following program will be green. On a black-and-white monitor, the shade will vary slightly from the dark background of the monitor screen.

Type the following. Be certain to type the commands exactly as they are listed to avoid bugs. Do not type the words in parentheses.

```
NEW
10 HOME
20 GR: COLOR = 4
30 HLIN 0,39 AT 0         (Type RUN and press
                          [RETURN] to see the
                          drawing, which is a
                          line at the top of the
                          screen.)
```

Now type LIST and press [RETURN] to continue writing the program. The listing will be at the bottom of the screen. If the line didn't appear when you typed RUN, check your listing carefully to make certain it is exactly the same as this manual.

```
40 HLIN 0,39 AT 39        (Type RUN and press
                          [RETURN] to see this
                          new line. Type LIST
                          and press [RETURN]
                          to continue
                          writing.)

50 VLIN 0,39 AT 0         (Type RUN to see
                          this line, then type
                          LIST to write the
                          next.)

60 VLIN 0,39 AT 39        (Type RUN to see
                          this line.)

70 END
```

Type RUN and press [RETURN] to see the entire program.

Draw a box in colors.

Now change the colors and add more lines to the box you drew from the preceding page. Remember to type RUN and press [RETURN] to see the program and type TEXT:HOME:LIST and press [RETURN] to list your program. From now on, only the directions "Run the program" or "List the program" will be given.

Type the following. (Don't type the explanations.)

```
NEW
10 HOME
20 REM DRAW A BOX USING VARIOUS COLORS AND
   DIVIDE IT INTO EQUAL SECTIONS

30 GR: COLOR = 6                        (GRAPHICS command:
                                        Color is blue.)

40 HLIN 0,39 AT 0                       (Top line in blue.)
50 HLIN 0,39 AT 39                      (Bottom line in
                                        blue.)

60 VLIN 0,39 AT 0                       (Left vertical line
                                        in blue.)

70 VLIN 0,39 AT 39                      (Right vertical line
                                        in blue.)

80 REM CHANGE THE COLOR TO YELLOW
90 COLOR = 13                           (This color command
                                        creates yellow.)

100 REM DIVIDE THE SCREEN INTO FOUR EQUAL
    SECTIONS

110 VLIN 0,39 AT 20                     (This draws a yellow
                                        vertical line at the
                                        center.)

120 HLIN 0,39 AT 20                     (This draws a yellow
                                        horizontal line at
                                        center.)

130 REM CHANGE THE COLOR TO RED AND DIVIDE
    THE SCREEN INTO EIGHT EQUAL SECTIONS

140 COLOR = 1                           (This color command
                                        creates red.)

150 VLIN 0,39 AT 10
160 VLIN 0,39 AT 30
170 HLIN 0,39 AT 10
180 HLIN 0,39 AT 30
```

Run the program.

Draw plots in your program.

Now add some plots to the drawing of the box from the preceding page. Type TEXT:HOME: and LIST to make certain the program is still in memory. Retype the program if necessary.

Here is the new section of the program:

```
190 REM CHANGE COLOR AND ADD PLOTS TO EACH
    SECTION
200  COLOR = 12 (This command creates
                  green.)
210 PLOT 5,5
```

Run the program to see the plot. Do this each time you want to see what's happening to the picture as the next lines are listed and run. Type TEXT:HOME:LIST and press [RETURN] to continue writing.

```
220 PLOT 15,5
230 PLOT 25,5
240 PLOT 35,5:PLOT 5,15:PLOT 5,25:5,35
250 PLOT 15,15: PLOT 15,25: PLOT 15,35
```

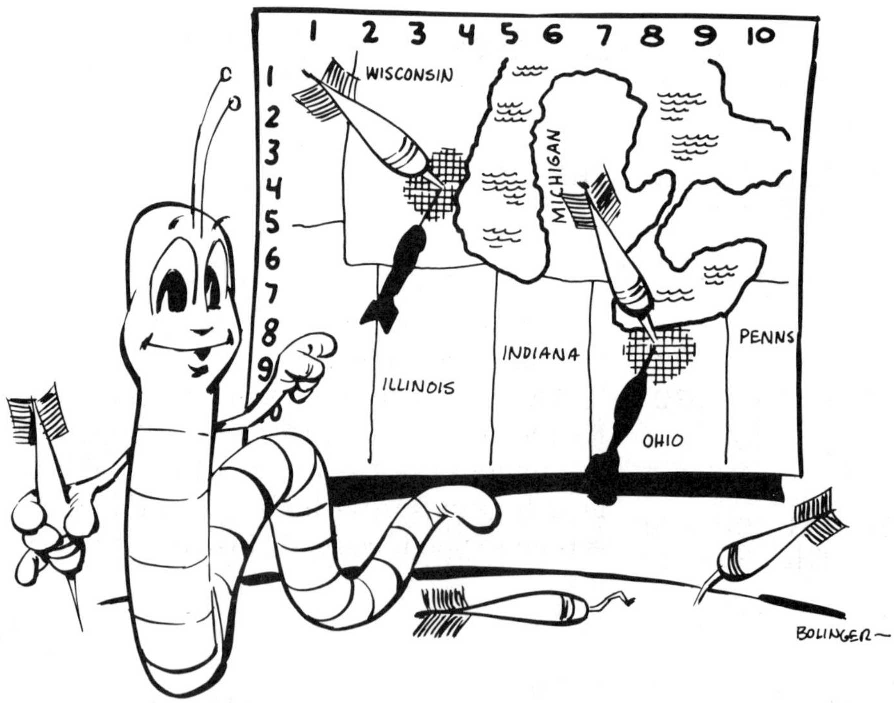

MILWAUKEE IS AT PLOT 4,4; CLEVELAND IS AT PLOT 8,9.

Several commands can be written on one line, separated by commas to save memory and time.

RUN the program to see all the new parts of the drawing.

Type the remaining lines.

```
260 PLOT 25,15:PLOT 25,25:PLOT 25,35
270 PLOT 35,15:PLOT 35,25:PLOT 35,35
280 END
```

RUN the program.

Change and add lines to the graphics program.

The horizontal lines in the program on the preceding pages will look neater if they are made shorter. An uneven look is created because the horizontal lines cross over the vertical lines with a slightly different pattern. Changing three lines in the program will correct this problem.

Type the following. Be certain the rest of the program is still in memory by typing TEXT:HOME: and LIST to see if the program is there. If it is not, retype the program and change Lines 120, 170, and 180.

```
120 HLIN 1,38 AT 20
170 HLIN 1,38 AT 10     (Starting at 1,
                         instead of 0, and
                         ending at 38,
                         instead of 39.)
180 HLIN 1,38 AT 30
```

Now RUN the program to see if it looks neater to you.

Now be creative and change some of the other lines to make new patterns and effects.

See what designs you can make by changing the lengths of HLIN and VLIN. Place some PLOT commands in different arrangements, without any HLIN and VLIN if you wish. Get thoroughly familiar with HLIN, VLIN, and PLOT and the size of the screen so you'll be ready to make the fancy and fun designs coming up!

Plan your program on paper.

It is advisable to make a paper sketch on a screen spacing chart to decide what to draw, where to place it, and how large to make it. Drawing on paper takes some of the guess work and trial and error out of graphics programming.

Select one of the easier suggestions listed below. After you've decided what you want to do, draw your idea on the screen spacing chart so you'll know exactly what it looks like and what spacing to use. Use a pencil so you can erase.

1. Draw a letter of the alphabet in graphics.
2. Draw a word using more than one letter.
3. Draw your initials.
4. Make a rectangle to represent a football field, putting in the necessary lines. (Do you like football?)
5. Draw the American flag.
6. Draw a fireplace; draw a stocking; draw a tree; draw a gift package. (Remind you of Christmas?)
7. Draw a Valentine heart.
8. Draw an Easter scene with a basket and bunny.
9. Draw a Halloween pumpkin.
10. Draw a Thanksgiving greeting.

When your sketch is finished, you will be ready to code your program in the BASIC language, so your computer can understand what you want it to do.

Learn to code your programs.

It is necessary to **code** your programs in a language that the computer can understand. Follow these steps to code a program that will draw the letter "A." First, draw the letter "A" so that it fits in the middle of the screen-spacing chart. Make it fill most of the screen vertically. Draw the top horizontal line of the "A" starting 3 lines down from the top and going from 16 to 29 horizontally. Be certain to use your screen-spacing chart for this program or these directions won't make much sense!

This line will be coded:

```
HLIN 16,29 at 3.
```

Draw the left vertical line of the "A" starting 3 spaces down from the top and 16 spaces to the right from the left margin, continuing down to 34 spaces from the top. This one will be coded:

```
VLIN 3,34 AT 16.
```

The right vertical line of the "A" will be the same length as the left vertical line, so it will be 3 down from the top and continue down to 34 spaces. However, it will be 29 spaces over from the left margin.

This will be coded:

```
VLIN 3,34 AT 29.
```

The middle line will run horizontally from 16 to 29 and be 20 lines down from the top. This line will be coded:

```
HLIN 16,29 AT 20.
```

Code your program after designing it on a chart.

After studying your screen spacing chart to see the arrangement of your drawing, you are ready to code the program. Write the program on paper, using line numbers.

First, clear the memory. (What command does this?)

```
NEW    (Don't give this command a line
       number!)
```

Next, clear the screen. (What command does this?)

```
10 HOME
```

Set graphics with GR. What always must be used with GR? That's right, the COLOR command!

```
20 GR: COLOR = 7
```

Now you are ready to put in the commands and numbers you figured from using the screen spacing chart. Give the HLIN and VLIN commands line numbers, and you'll be ready to RUN!

```
30 HLIN 16,29 AT 3
40 VLIN 3,34 AT 16
50 VLIN 3,34 AT 29
60 HLIN 16,29 AT 20
```

What comes at the end of a program? That's correct . . .

```
70 END
```

Now you are ready to type in the program and get your big "A" grade for your good work!

As you can see, some of your programming can be done away from the computer. You can preplan before you actually type in the program at the computer. This preplanning can save you a great deal of time and frustration! You can start working on a program even when you aren't sitting at a computer. This is called desk top programming. Everything starts in your own mind when you are working with a computer!

Use a FOR-NEXT loop to repeat lines in graphics.

It is possible to use FOR-NEXT in graphics to draw related lines. Whatever command or action that comes between FOR and NEXT will be repeated the number of times indicated by the variable. The STEP command indicates the number of steps or spaces between the lines of the drawing. FOR-NEXT automatically gives an increment step of 1 unless the STEP command indicates a different increment. In this program, the increment is 39 spaces, because the command is STEP 39.

Study and type this program:

```
NEW
10 HOME
15 GR:COLOR = 12
20 FOR Y = 0 TO 39 STEP 39
```

The loop will go from 0 to 39. The command STEP 39 makes the computer go directly from 0 to 39 and skip the numbers in between.

```
30 VLIN 0,39 AT Y
```

Two vertical lines will be printed—one at 0 and one at 39 because this line in the program is located in the middle of a FOR-NEXT loop with a STEP 39.

```
40 NEXT Y

50 FOR X = 0 TO 39 STEP 39

60 HLIN 1,39 AT X
70 NEXT X

80 END
```

Now RUN the program to see what happens.

Experiment using the STEP command with various numbers.

Change the STEP command in the program on the preceding page to make different arrangements of the lines. Retype the following line. Remember: never put a comma before the STEP command!

```
20 FOR Y = 0 TO 39 STEP 3
```

Now, there will be lines every three spaces because of the STEP 3 command.

RUN the program to see all the new lines!

Retype this line:

```
50 FOR X = 0 TO 39 STEP 3
```

Now RUN the program to see all the new horizontal lines.

Retype this again if you want the lines to start on the right margin and go down one increment each time, using a negative step.

```
20 FOR Y = 39 TO 0 STEP -1
```

The same thing can be done with the horizontal lines.

```
50 FOR X = 39 TO 0 STEP -1
```

Experiment with other STEP increments. FOR-NEXT and STEP commands will make more sense to you as you continue to work with them. (That's a promise.) Anything you keep doing becomes easier and more understandable.

Don't ever give up trying to master a computer . . . or yourself!

"Mental growing pains" can be painful . . . but it's worth the effort!

By this time, you might feel a bit overwhelmed by all of these new commands and ideas. This happens to people who are trying to learn something new. It could be called "mental growing pains."

When you feel a little discouraged, go back and take a look at the goals you set for yourself in Chapter 1. Remind yourself that all this work and frustration is worth the price! You set goals for yourself. You will reach your goals if you keep working.

Remember: **Experts are beginnners who never gave up!**

Be certain to save the program on the next page on a disk so you can run it whenever you need to be reminded to keep your faith in yourself and never give up!

HAVE FAITH IN YOURSELF TO REACH YOUR GOAL!

Study and type the "I have faith in me!" program.

Type carefully and proofread as you go along. Make corrections as you complete each section. After typing the last line in a section, run and test the program to see the letter you've made. Then type TEXT:HOME:LIST to continue typing the program. Make any necessary corrections before going to the next section of the program.

```
NEW

10 HOME
20 GR:COLOR = 3
30 REM I HAVE FAITH IN ME!

40 REM THE LETTER "F"
50 VLIN 12,28 AT 5
60 HLIN 5,9 AT 12
70 HLIN 5,8 AT 20

80 REM THE LETTER "A"
90 VLIN 12,28 AT 12
100 HLIN 12,16 AT 12
110 VLIN 12,28 AT 16
120 HLIN 12,16 AT 20

130 REM THE LETTER "I"
140 VLIN 12,28 AT 19

150 REM THE LETTER "T"
160 VLIN 12,28 AT 24
170 HLIN 22,26 at 12
```

```
180 REM THE LETTER "H"
190 VLIN 12,28 AT 29
200 VLIN 12,28 AT 33
210 HLIN 29,33, AT 20

220 REM CLOSING LINES IN TEXT WINDOW
230 HTAB 3
240 PRINT: "I HAVE FAITH IN MY ABILITY TO
    LEARN."
```

Type RUN to see the entire program.

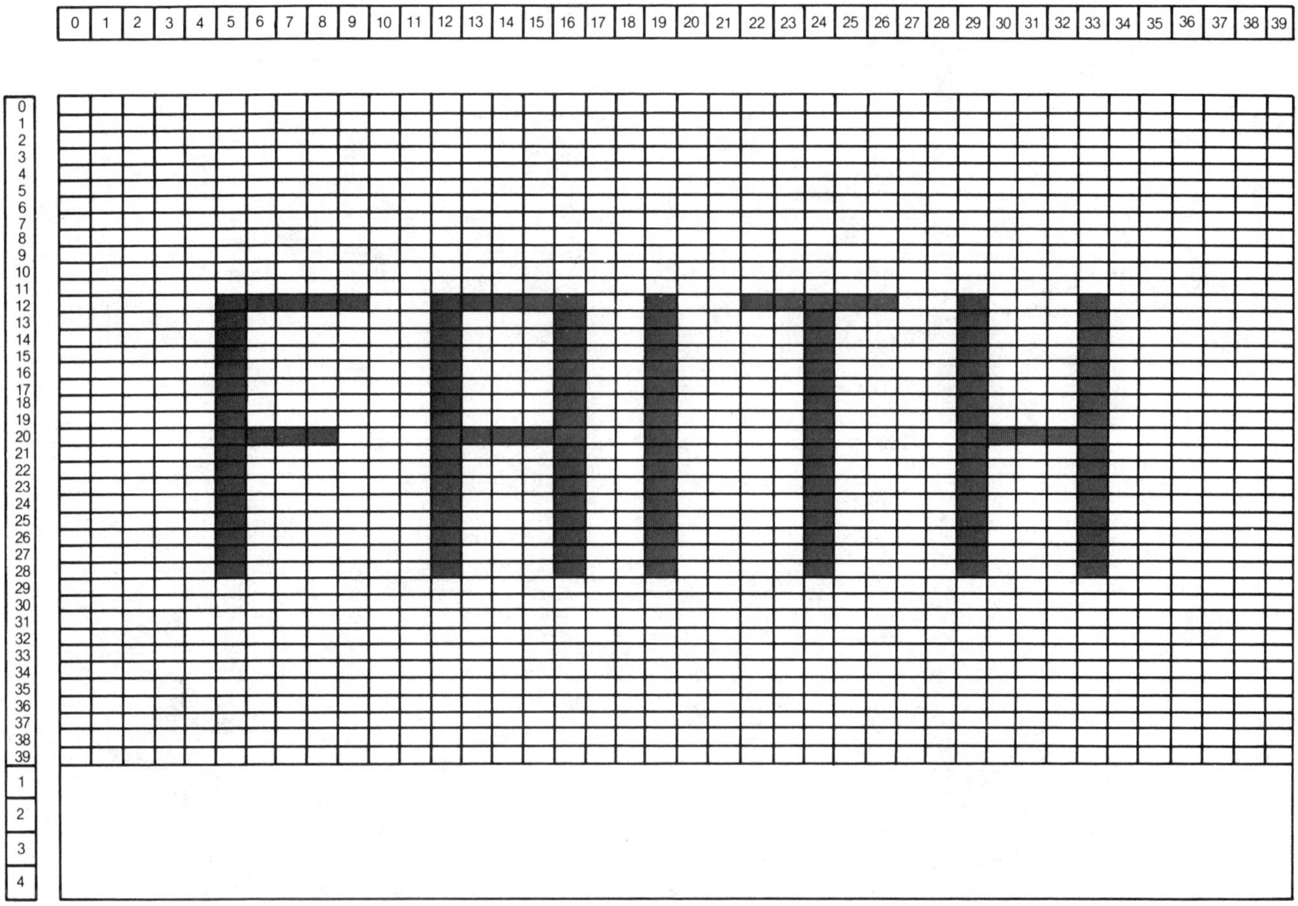

Learn to use the HGR command for high resolution.

High resolution graphics drawings can have much finer detail than low resolution graphics. The screen pixels are much smaller, which allows for much finer lines and plots.

HGR is the command used for setting high resolution graphics.

Horizontal locations are numbered from 0 to 279, starting with zero (0) at the left edge of the screen and ending with 279 over at the right edge of the screen.

Vertical pixels are numbered from zero (0) to 159, starting with zero (0) at the top of the screen and going down to 159 at the bottom of the screen. HGR leaves an area called a **text window** on the bottom of the screen which is reserved for text. The command HGR2 erases the text window and utilizes the entire vertical screen, changing it to 191 vertical spaces possible.

Study the high resolution graphics chart.

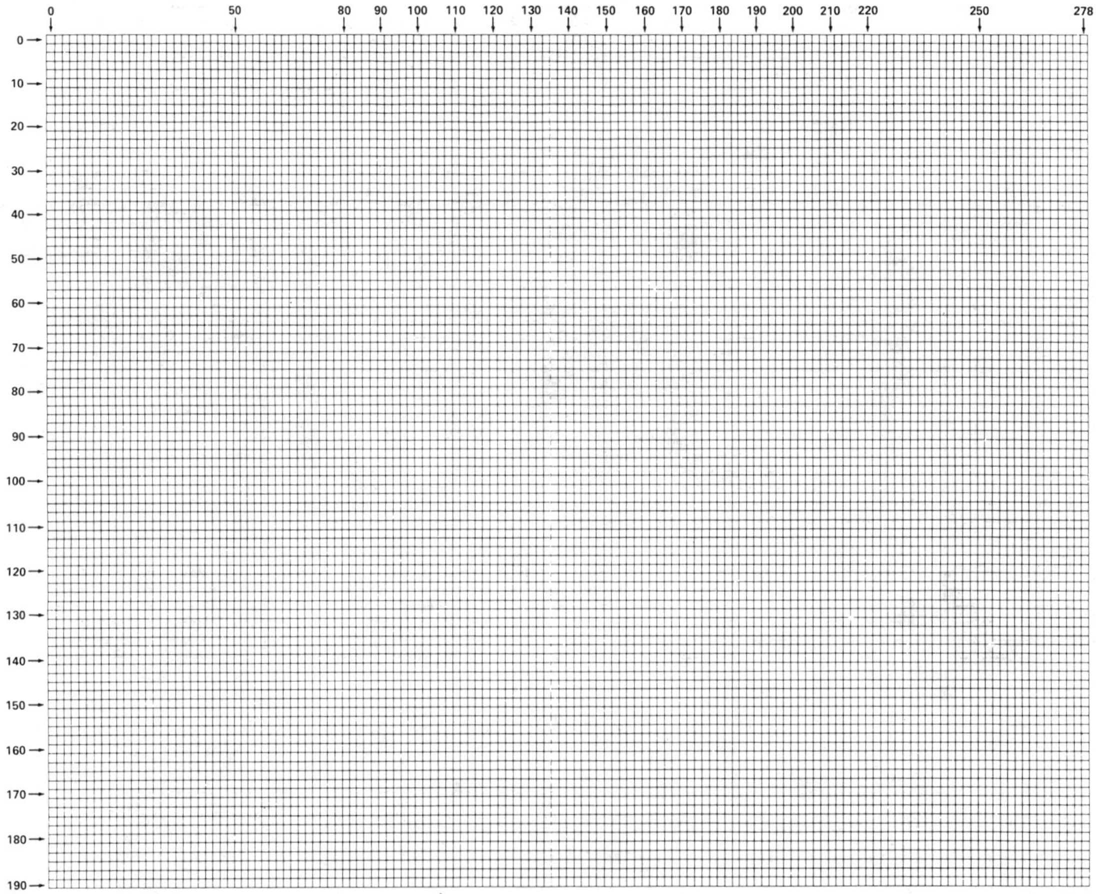

HIGH RESOLUTION SCREEN LAYOUT

Learn to use colors with high resolution graphics.

There aren't as many colors available for high resolution graphics as there are for low resolution graphics. The command HCOLOR, which brings up the color for high resolution graphics, stands for high resolution color. Notice, there are two different numbers for both black and white.

The HCOLORS are numbered from 0 to 7.

0 = BLACK	4 = BLACK
1 = GREEN	5 = ORANGE
2 = VIOLET	6 = BLUE
3 = WHITE	7 = WHITE

Certain colors don't draw vertical lines on black-and white monitors. Colors 2 and 6 only plot vertical lines beginning with even numbers; colors 1 and 5 only plot lines beginning with odd numbers. When you are programming in GRAPHICS and the vertical lines don't appear, change either the color or the number so the vertical lines can be printed.

LOW RESOLUTION OFFERS MORE COLORS.

Learn to use high resolution graphics (HGR).

High resolution graphics has approximately seven times as many horizontal and four times as many vertical pixels as low resolution graphics.

Drawing lines is easier in HGR because diagonal lines can be made, and many lines can be connected using one command.

HPLOT, the command used for drawing in HGR, is always followed by two numbers. The first number is the beginning horizontal location—the second number is the beginning vertical location.

For example, HPLOT 0,10 would plot the position at zero, or at the left margin horizontally, and down 10 spaces from the top vertically.

Draw lines using high resolution graphics.

To draw a line using high resolution graphics, two points must be connected, giving the horizontal and vertical positions of both sets of numbers. Study and type the following.

```
NEW
10 HOME

20 HGR:HCOLOR = 3           (Color will be
                            WHITE.)

30 HPLOT 0,0 TO 279,0
```

The beginning horizontal and vertical location comes first; then the word TO, followed by the ending horizontal and vertical location.

Line 30 will draw the top line.

```
40 HPLOT 0,159 TO 279,159
```

Line 40 will draw the bottom line on the screen.

```
50 HPLOT 0,0 TO 0,159
```

Line 50 will draw the left vertical line.

```
60 HPLOT 279,0 TO 279,159
```

Line 60 will draw the right vertical line.

Run the program.

Draw diagonal lines using high resolution graphics.

Diagonal lines may be drawn by connecting diagonal points. Study and type the following.

```
NEW
10 HOME
20 HGR2:HCOLOR = 1
30 HPLOT 0,0 to 279,159   (Left upper
                          corner to right
                          lower corner.)
```

```
40 HPLOT 279,0 TO 0,159   (Upper right
                           corner to lower
                           left.)
```

Run the program to see the diagonal lines.

HPLOTS may be typed together to save time and space.

Study and type the following example.

```
NEW
10 HOME
20 HGR2:HCOLOR = 3
30 HPLOT 0,0 TO 279,0 TO 279,159
35 HPLOT 0,159 TO 0,0
40 END
```

When plots are "chained together," the last number of the preceding plot becomes the beginning number of the next plot. For example, HPLOT 0,0 TO 279,0 TO 279,159 is the same as:

```
HPLOT 0,0 TO 279,0: HPLOT 279,0 TO 279,159
```

The repeated plot, (279,0), is omitted. It is still in memory; the computer can continue on from that area, even though it is not rewritten in the program.

Rewrite and upgrade some of your programs.

Now that you know some of the differences between low resolution graphics and high resolution graphics, you should be able to write programs in either style.

Rewrite one or more of the programs from this chapter using FOR-NEXT loops for duplicated actions, or change a program you wrote in low resolution to high resolution graphics linking some commands together to make diagonal lines. Always try to upgrade your programs to improve your style of writing.

Egoless programming, being able to be open and objective about trying to make your programs better, should be one of your goals. In the early days, programs were considered to be works of art. Most programmers didn't want anyone to suggest changes or improvements to their projects. Programs were extremely difficult to understand. Now, however, most programs are written in a very clear and concise manner.

Write your programs so that anyone with training can understand what you are trying to accomplish. If someone offers suggestions to improve your programs, accept this help with gratitude.

Consistently strive to become a better programmer. Review and edit some of your earlier programs to make them even better than they first were.

You always come out the winner when you compete with yourself and strive for excellence.

ALL OF MY PROGRAMS ARE "EGOLESS."

The Apple Mouse can be used on Apple computers.

The Apple **Mouse** is a small mechanical peripheral that rolls across a desk top on a small rubber ball. As the ball moves, the cursor on the screen also moves. The Mouse can be attached to all of the Apple models mentioned in this book if they have enough memory to hold the necessary software instructions.

The Apple IIc has a portal located at the back of the computer where the Mouse is connected. A special card must be inserted inside the Apple IIe, II Plus, or Apple II.

The Mouse offers much greater variety and ease than the keyboard for preparing drawings and graphics. The total price for the Apple Mouse and the software called MousePaint is priced under $100. It is well worth the money! The Apple Mouse and MousePaint can help you produce drawings, charts, lettering and cards. Delightful effects can be created using simulated drawing tools such as a pencil, paint brush, or a spray can. Don't these descriptions of various effects sound interesting?

Computer technology is giving us an opportunity to be more creative. Using a Mouse is a great way to produce graphics for many purposes.

Printing graphics requires special software programs.

It is necessary to use special programs to print graphics hard copy. Some printers cannot reproduce graphics; however, the program lines can be listed on all printers.

Check with the manual of your printer to learn how to work with graphics. Call the person who sold your hardware to you, if necessary, to find out what software is required to print drawings, graphs, or charts on your particular equipment.

You may wish to become more expert by reading some of the many books and magazines dealing with computer art. Experiment and learn all you can. Learning to use low and high resolution graphics can help you learn to control the computer and better understand how a computer functions.

OF COURSE, IF YOUR PRINTER WON'T PRINT GRAPHICS, IT'S BACK TO THE DRAWING BOARD.

VOCABULARY TO REMEMBER

BASIC commands

GR Command used to bring low resolution graphics to the screen.

HLIN Command used to plot horizontal lines in in low resolution graphics.

VLIN Command used to plot vertical lines in low resolution graphics.

PLOT Command used with low resolution graphics to indicate a horizontal and vertical location.

COLOR = Command which must be used with low resolution graphics to indicate which of 16 colors is to be used.

TEXT Screen output in alphanumeric characters.

STEP Command used with FOR-NEXT to indicate increments other than one.

HGR Command used to bring high resolution graphics to the monitor screen. This command allows for a text window at the bottom of the screen, leaving 160 vertical plotting points.

HGR2 Command for high resolution graphics which removes the text window from the bottom of the screen making room for 192 vertical plotting points.

HCOLOR= Command used with high resolution graphics to select a color.

HPLOT Command used with high resolution graphics to state beginning and ending horizontal and vertical plots.

Terms

Graphics Information presented in the form of pictures or images on the screen or on hard copy.

Low Resolution Graphics Graphics display with 16 available colors; the display area is 40 columns both horizontally and vertically.

Pixels Small squares on the screen which are formed by a network of vertical and horizontal lines.

Text Window Spaces which are left on a graphics display screen to allow for text characters to be printed.

High Resolution Graphics Graphics display with 6 colors. There are 280 columns across and 192 rows vertically. With the text window, the display area is 280 by 160. HGR is the command which reserves the text window. HGR2 utilizes the entire screen.

Code To write program commands in a language that can be understood by the computer.

Mouse Small mouse-sized device used with a computer to create graphics and charts.

CREATIVE CORNER

Graphics can be lots of fun when you get the knack of it, and I'm certain you'll enjoy using your Apple even more now that you've learned how to make drawings on your screen.

Here are some review questions to make certain you've got the main ideas. Check back in the chapter if you can't remember some of the details.

1. Which direction is horizontal?
2. Which direction is vertical?
3. How many horizontal spaces are available in low resolution graphics?
4. How many vertical spaces are available in low resolution graphics with a text window on the screen? Without a text window?
5. What are the two commands necessary to begin low resolution graphics?
6. What are the two commands used to draw horizontal and vertical lines in low resolution graphics?
7. What command is used for high resolution graphics?
8. Where would PLOT 8,22 be located on the screen?
9. How is a screen spacing chart helpful?
10. What is coding, and why is it necessary?
11. What is the difference between text and graphics?
12. Where would HPLOT 0,0 TO 279,159 be located on the screen?
13. What are pixels?
14. How is a mouse used with a computer?
15. What is MousePaint?

9
ARITHMETIC—COMPUTER STYLE!

GOAL: To learn to do arithmetic on the Apple computer.

THOUGHT: When you control your thoughts, you control your life!

Aa Bb Cc Dd Ee Ff Gg Hh Ii Jj Kk Ll Mm

Vocabulary To Learn:

BASIC Commands: SPEED =

TERMS:

MATH OPERATORS	RELATIONAL OPERATORS	RESERVED WORDS
EXPONENTIATION	CONDITIONAL BRANCHING	TRUNCATION
PRECEDENCE		

A computer can do math rapidly and accurately.

The simplest method to use in doing computer-style math is to write the command PRINT—followed by numbers which are to be multiplied, divided, added, subtracted, or raised to a power—connected by one or more of the **math operators**.

The math operators are:

* Multiplication
/ Division
+ Addition
− Subtraction
^ Exponentiation (raising to a power)

Locate these symbols on your keyboard. Turn back to Chapter 4 if you've forgotten the correct fingers to use. It's very important to keep using good keyboarding technique.

Use immediate mode with PRINT.

When you want just the answer to a math problem, type in the numbers along with a math operator (+, −, *, /, or ^) after a PRINT statement. Do not use the equal sign. When the program is run, the answer will be there. Practice typing some equations.

```
PRINT 22 - 15
```

Press [RETURN]. Voila! There's the answer!

When using immediate execution (when no line numbers are written), the answer will be given only once. In delayed execution (with line numbers) the equation can be repeated as often as desired because it is stored in memory.

```
NEW
10 HOME
20 PRINT 2 + 2
```

RUN the program.
(The number 4 will appear by itself on the screen. The computer will add 2 + 2, then print only the answer.)

Here's another example to help make this problem more understandable:

```
20 PRINT "THE ANSWER TO 2 + 2 IS "; 2 + 2
```

This time the literal in quotes, THE ANSWER TO 2 + 2 IS, will be printed. The semicolon instructs the computer to stay on the same line. Then the equation following the semicolon 2 + 2 is processed, and only the answer is printed.

Study and type the following:

```
NEW
10 HOME
20 PRINT 8 * 8 (Just the answer will be
              printed.)
30 PRINT "EIGHT TIMES EIGHT IS "; 8 * 8
40 PRINT 12 / 6
50 PRINT "TWELVE DIVIDED BY 6 IS "; 12 / 6
   (The entire sentence will be printed.)
```

Run the program to see computer-style math!

Run separate lines in a program to see if they work.

It is possible to see the results of some lines without running the entire program. Simply type RUN before the line number and press [RETURN].

Here is an example:

```
NEW
10 HOME
20 PRINT 5 * 5
30 PRINT "6 TIMES 7 = "; 6 * 7
```

If you want to see Line 20, type:

```
RUN 20
```

If you want to see Line 30, type:

```
RUN 30
```

Check for type errors as you finish each line.

It is easier to find errors, which are called "bugs" in computer jargon, if you check each line right after you have typed it. That makes it possible to correct mistakes immediately. Since most of your bugs will come from typing errors, it is very important to keep developing good keyboard technique. Review Chapter 4 and frequently check your position at the computer. Continue to use the correct fingers for all alphabet, numbers, and symbols.

IT'S EASIER TO FIND "BUGS" IF YOU CHECK EACH LINE RIGHT AFTER YOU HAVE TYPED IT.

Print blank spaces in literals to make copy readable.

Study and type this line again:

```
30 PRINT "6 TIMES 7 IS "; 6 * 7
```

Notice that a space is left before the last quotation in Line 30. This allows for a space to be left between "IS" and the answer, 42. Otherwise the sentence would look like this:

6 TIMES 7 IS42. (That doesn't look neat and is difficult to read. Right?) Use correct spacing when you write your programs.

Math operators are processed in the order of priority.

In doing math, the computer gives a certain order of priority to the math operators. They must "wait their turn" to be processed, if there is more than one operator in an equation.

Precedence (pronounced "PRE - SEE - DENCE") and priority have similar meanings. They both refer to what goes first in order. You use precedence everyday as you decide "What shall I do first?" You have to first get out of bed, then get dressed, before you go anywhere in the morning. Wouldn't it be funny if you had someone push your bed to school or work because you didn't give getting out of bed precedence?

EX—PO—NEN—SI—A—SHUN? EX—PO—NEN—TI—A—TION?
HOW DO YOU SPELL THAT LONG WORD?

Numbers with parentheses are first in order of priority.

1. Any numbers within parentheses are given top priority over any other numbers in the equation.

For example: (4 − 2) ∗ (3 + 4)
4 − 2 = 2 would be figured first;
then 3 + 4 = 7
and finally 2 ∗ 7 = 14

In other words, the answers to the problems within the parentheses become the main numbers to be multiplied.

Type this line and see if "14" matches the answer that the computer gets doing computer-style math.

```
PRINT (4 - 2) * (3 + 4)
```

Press [RETURN].

Exponentiation comes next in order of priority.

2. Using **exponentiation**, a number is multiplied by itself the number of times indicated after the exponentiation sign. This sign looks like a tiny tepee placed between numbers. For example:

```
4 + 3 ^ 2 (This would be 3 "squared.")
```

The number 3 is to be first multiplied by itself (3 times 3)—making 9. Then 9 would be added to 4; so the answer would be 9 plus 4 equals 13.

Type this problem on the computer.

```
PRINT 4 + 3 ^ 2
```

(Press [RETURN].) Was the answer 13? Good!

Get better acquainted with EX - PO - NEN - TI - A - TION.

Exponentiation . . . phew! There are 14 letters in that long word! It is a mouthful! Pronounce it slowly, syllable by syllable. Say EX - PO - NEN - TI- A- TION. (It sounds like "EX - PO - NEN - SHE - A - SHUN.", but don't spell it that way!) Say it many times to get acquainted with this long, strange, important new word. Write it several times now, making certain to say it in syllables as you spell it. (Use this method to learn new words that seem difficult. New words and ideas are always easier if you take them one step at a time.)

Now type a problem using exponentiation:

```
PRINT 5 ^ 2 - 3 (Press [RETURN].)
```

Five multiplied by itself equals 25. Then subtract 3 from 25. The answer is 22. Did you get that?

Exponentiation will become easier the more you use it. Anything you keep doing correctly becomes more enjoyable and easier to do!

Multiplication and division come next in order of priority.

3. Multiplication and division follow exponentiation. They are given equal order of priority, reading from left to right in an equation. (Remember: the asterisk (*) is used instead of "X" to indicate multiplication.)

Study this example:

```
7 * 7 + 4
```

This would be 7 times 7, making 49, plus 4 would equal 53.
Type it on the computer:

```
PRINT 7 * 4 + 4 (Press [RETURN].)
```

Remember the slash (/) is used instead of the standard division sign to indicate division. Read all equations from left to right.

Study and type the following:

```
PRINT 3 * 4 / 2 (Press [RETURN].)
```

The multiplication would occur first. Three times 4 equals 12. The 12 would then be divided by 2, making the answer 6.

Try another problem. First do it in your mind; then check it on the computer to see if you did it correctly.

```
PRINT 4 / 2 * 7
```

MATH OPERATORS MUST BE IN ORDER.

This time the division would come first, reading from left to right. So 4 divided by 2 is 2; then multiplying by 7 would give the answer of 14. Did you get the right answer?

Addition and subtraction come last in order of priority.

4. Addition and subtraction have equal precedence, following all other math operators reading from left to right.

Study and type the following:

```
PRINT 4 + 8 / 8
```

This problem looks like it might be 4 plus 8, making 12, divided by 8, which would make an answer of 1 1/2. Using precedence, the 8 is first divided by 8, which equals 1. Then 4 is added to the 1, making the final answer 5.

Now study this problem with subtraction, reading from left to right:

```
PRINT  3 - 2 + 7 * 10
```

The multiplication would be done first: 7 times 10 equals 70. Then reading from left to right, 3 - 2 equals 1. Then add 1 plus 70, making the answer 71.

Learn the precedence of math operators

To summarize what you have learned about precedence or order of priority of math operators, study the following list.

The computer will read math operators in this order:

1. Parentheses—Any numbers with operators enclosed in parentheses will get figured first.

   ```
   PRINT  (3 + 4) * 8
   ```

   (Three plus 4 equals 7 times 8 equals 56.)
2. Exponentiation—Any number with a ^ operator will be given second precedence, reading from left to right.

   ```
   PRINT 6 + 3 ^ 2
   ```

   The number 3 times itself or squared equals 9, plus 6 equals 15.

3. Multiplication and division—(* and / operators are given equal third precedence, reading from left to right.)

```
PRINT 6 * 8 / 4
```

(Six times 8 equals 48 divided by 4 is 12.)

4. Addition and subtraction—(+ and − operators are given equal fourth precedence, reading from left to right.

```
PRINT 10 - 4 + 7
```

(Ten minus 4 equals 6 plus 7 equals 13.)

Now you can do all kinds of math problems with these operators. Developing good skills in arithmetic is very important, so learn all you can and become more expert.

Inner parentheses are processed before outer parentheses.

If there are parentheses within parentheses, the computer will figure the innermost (inside) parentheses first.

Here is an example:

```
12 / (3 + (1 + 2) ^ 2)
```

The inner parentheses contains (1 + 2) which equals 3. Now the problem reads:

```
12 / (3 = 3 ^ 2)
```

Now the other numbers inside the outer parentheses can be figured. First would come the exponentiation: 3 ^ 2 would be 3 times itself, or 3 squared, which equals 9. Now the problem reads:

```
12 / ( 3 + 9)
```

Now the numbers inside the parentheses can be added:

```
3 + 9 = 12
```

Now the problem is 12 / 12 (12 divided by 12), which is 1, so the answer to 12 / (3 + (1 + 2) ^ 2) is 1.

When this problem is broken down in small sections, it isn't difficult at all. Again, take one step at a time in learning. Anything is easier when it is correctly done in small sections!

Be very careful as you type math programs.

Now carefully type the problem into the computer.

Be certain to get every figure correct and the parentheses in the correct positions. Carefully type one character at a time.

```
PRINT 12 / (3 + (1 + 2) ^ 2)
```

Now press [RETURN]. If everything was entered in correctly, you should have a beautiful 1 on your screen, meaning you are a number one typist!

Follow directions, and be more accurate than you've ever been in your life if you want to be successful at operating a computer. You can't afford to be sloppy or make mistakes. It is quicker to do it slowly and correctly the first time instead of trying to type very fast and making lots of mistakes. Learn to read copy l-e-t-t-e-r by l-e-t-t-e-r when you are trying to make perfect copy. This is especially important for programming commands and typing figures and symbols.

Study the following and figure the answers. Then carefully type them to check your answers . . . and your typing!

```
PRINT 44 / (2 + 2)
PRINT (44 / 2) + 2
PRINT 3 + (-2 * 2)
PRINT (3 - 2) * 2
PRINT 100 / (200 / (1 * (9 - 5)))
```

(Remember to first do the math in the inside parentheses, if you're doing your own figuring!)

The answers are: 11, 24, − 1, 2, 2

Relational operators are used to make comparisons.

In addition to being able to make rapid and accurate arithmetic computations, the computer can be used to make comparisons, which is extremely useful in many ways. The computer can judge whether one amount is the same size as, larger than, or smaller than another amount.

Six symbols are used in Applesoft BASIC to make comparisons. They are sometimes called **relational operators**. Study the following table:

RELATIONAL OPERATORS

MEANING OF OPERATOR	SYMBOL
EQUAL TO	=
GREATER THAN	>
LESS THAN	<
GREATER THAN OR EQUAL TO	>=
LESS THAN OR EQUAL TO	<=
NOT EQUAL TO	<>

Relational operators are used in making decisions.

When using the relational operators to make a decision the computer indicates True with the number 1, and False with the number zero (0).

Have you ever given signals, like "Knock once for Yes and twice for No"? The computer does almost the same thing. It makes a signal with the number 1 to indicate True, and a signal using a zero (0) to indicate False.

REMEMBER: 1 STANDS FOR TRUE; 0 STANDS FOR FALSE.

Study and type the following, which are all true statements. The computer will print a 1 if they are typed in and processed.

```
PRINT 5 = 5     (5 is equal to 5.)
PRINT 7 < 8     (7 is less than 8.)
PRINT 10 > 9    (10 is greater than 9.)
PRINT 4 = 4     (4 is equal to 4.)
PRINT 32 < 33   (32 is less than 33.)
PRINT 3 <> 4    (3 is not equal to 4.)
PRINT 5 <= 6    (5 is less than or equal to 6.)
PRINT 3 >= 2    (3 is greater than or equal to 2.)
```

The computer indicates false by printing a zero.

Study and type the following, which will all be false:

```
PRINT 3 = 1      (3 is not equal to 1.)
PRINT 78 > 124 (78 is not greater than 124.)
PRINT 10 < 9     (10 is not less than 9.)
PRINT 32 <> 32 (32 is not equal to 32.)
PRINT 32 <= 30 (32 is not less than or equal to 30.)
PRINT 4 >= 8     (4 is not greater than or equal to 8.)
```

All of these are false, so the computer will print a 0 to communicate this information to the user. The computer doesn't mean that the user is a zero. So don't get your feelings hurt if you see a zero on the screen. You're Number 1 if you've stuck with learning about computers this far. Hurray for you!

Math and relational operators can be used with IF THEN statements. If a condition meets a certain requirement, an action takes place. For example: IF 3 + 2 = 5 THEN PRINT "YES, 3 + 2 = 5." The computer makes a decision, and then it does an action based on that decision.

Have you ever been told "If you get your work finished, then you can go"? This is a similar situation to a computer relational operator determining an action that is to follow. Most everything a computer does is based on logic which comes from "a thrilling, real-life situation." (Sounds like daytime T.V.!)

Relational operators are used for conditional branching.

If a condition meets a certain requirement, **conditional branching** takes place. The computer goes to a line or does some kind of action out of the normal ascending order of reading line numbers. Conditional branching can be used for many types of applications.

Variables are used with math and relational operators.

Variables are used to represent amounts that can be compared on the computer before **conditional branching** can take place. Study and type the following:

```
NEW
10 HOME
20 A = 3                          (The variable A is assigned the
                                  value of 3.)
30 B = 5                          (The variable B is assigned the
                                  value of 5.)
40 C = A + B                      (The variable C is equal to the
                                  sum of A and B.)
50 IF C = 8 THEN GO TO 70         (This is a CONDITIONAL BRANCH. If
                                  the variable C equals 8, the
                                  computer will go to Line 70 and
                                  skip Line 60.)
60 IF C <> 8 THEN GOTO 80         (This is another CONDITIONAL
                                  BRANCH. If C does not equal 8,
                                  the computer will go to the END,
                                  Line 80, and not print Line 70.)
70 PRINT "YES, 3 + 5 DOES EQUAL 8."
80 END
```

RUN the program.

NOW I KNOW WHAT VARIABLE MEANS.

An ability to solve math story problems is helpful.

Most of the arithmetic done in programming is similar to solving story problems. It is necessary to "think through" a problem to decide whether to use addition, subtraction, multiplication, exponentiation, or relational operators.

Certain equations or formulas are used in doing arithmetic on computers. For instance, here is one that figures the time it takes to travel somewhere when distance and rate of speed are known.

The equation is TIME = DISTANCE DIVIDED BY SPEED.

If you are going to drive 50 miles an hour for 200 miles, it would take you four hours. Here is how it's figured:

DISTANCE = 200
SPEED = 50
DISTANCE / SPEED = TIME
TIME IS THE SAME AS 200 / 50 OR 4 HOURS.

Variables can be assigned to represent distance, speed, and time. The closer the variable name resembles the actual term, the easier it is to recognize what it represents. Many times, the word itself can act as a variable name, unless any of its letters are reserved as a special command word. The computer uses only the first two letters of a variable to distinguish it from others; the variable will break up on the screen into sections if any part of it is one of the **reserved words**. A syntax error appears in the line that this occurs. Everyone has this happen sooner or later.

Reserved words are listed in the back of this manual.

A variable may be assigned to a descriptive word.

It is possible to use the word TIME as a variable to represent itself, because its letters T-I-M-E aren't part of a command or reserved word. However, both SPEED and DISTANCE contain letters that are part of reserved words.

In fact, the word SPEED= is a command which regulates how fast a program is listed or run. The normal rate is SPEED = 255. If you want your program to list at a slow rate of speed, or if you want it to output at a slower rate than normal, type SPEED = 100 or whatever speed you wish, just as long as it isn't faster than 255, or slower than 1. SPEED = may be given a line number and be included as part of a program, or it may be given as an immediate execution command.

COME ON. . .THE SNAIL IS WINNING!

WOW! YOU CAN REALLY GOOOOO!

Speed doesn't function in a graphics program.

DISTANCE contains letters which are reserved commands, so this word cannot be used as a variable.

Assign variables and describe them in REM statements.

So let's compromise and use TIME to represent how long the trip will take; S to represent SPEED, and DST to represent DISTANCE.

Now the equation will look like this:

TIME = DST / S (Time is distance divided by the rate of speed.)

The equation is still understandable and won't interfere with any reserved words. These are the variables to be used:

TIME = TIME
S = RATE OF SPEED
DST = DISTANCE

It is efficient programming to describe the variables in REM statements or in a documentation section of the program, so that the program is more understandable.

Study and type the following:

```
NEW
10 HOME
20 REM TIME = DISTANCE / RATE OF SPEED
30 REM TIME = TIME, S = SPEED, DST =
   DISTANCE
40 DST = 100
50 S = 20
60 TIME = DST / S
70 PRINT "WHEN TRAVELING "; DST; " MILES"
80 PRINT "AT THE SPEED OF ";S
90 PRINT "IT WILL TAKE ";TIME; " HOURS."
100 END
```

Type RUN and press [RETURN].

In Lines 70, 80, and 90, the literals are in quotes and will be printed exactly as they are written. The variables are not in quotes, because the numbers they represent replace the variables when the program is run.

Write programs from story problems.

This same type of program can be used for figuring many distances and speeds. Here are story problems that can be solved by using this equation.

1. If a man drove his car 40 miles an hour, traveling from Phoenix to San Diego, which is about 360 miles, what time would he arrive if he left Monday morning at 8?

   TIME = DISTANCE/RATE OF SPEED

   (Can you do the rest now and figure out what time he would reach his destination?)
2. A plane flew between New York and Los Angeles at a speed of 400 miles per hour. How long did it take? (It is about 2000 miles from the Atlantic Coast to the Pacific Coast.)
3. Here is another type of problem which deals with money. A girl bought 3 dresses which cost $35 each. She gave the clerk a check for $150. How much change did she receive?

   Here is the equation for this problem:

   CHANGE RECEIVED = PAYMENT − (PRICE TIMES QUANTITY)

The change received is equal to the amount of payment, minus the price of each article, times the quantity. (Cash registers are set up with programs that are similar to this one.)

Now write programs that will solve these problems.

CASH REGISTERS HAVE PROGRAMS SIMILAR TO THIS ONE.

Here is an example of the "CHANGE" program.

Here is one way to write the "CHANGE" program from the preceding page. Study it, then type it into your computer.

```
NEW
10  HOME
20 REM FIGURING CHANGE PROGRAM

30 REM CHANGE = PMT - (COST TIMES QTY.)
```

(The change is equal to the amount of the payment, minus the cost, times the number of items purchased.)

```
40 REM  CGE = CHANGE, PMT = PAYMENT
```

(CGE will represent the amount of change; PMT will represent the amount of payment.)

```
50 REM  CST = COST, AMT = QUANTITY
```

(CST will represent the cost; AMT will represent quantity.)

```
60 CST = 35
```

(The Cost variable is assigned 35.)

```
70 AMT = 3
```

(The Quantity variable is assigned 3.)

```
80 PMT = 150
```

(The payment variable is assigned 150.)

```
90 CGE = PMT - (CST * AMT)
```

(Math equation. See Line 30.)

```
100 PRINT "YOUR CHANGE IS "; CGE
```

(Prints the literal with the amount of change.)

RUN and press [RETURN].

Experiment using different amounts for the variables representing cost, payment, amount, etc.

Learn to use truncation to round off numbers.

To round off numbers so that there won't be a string of numbers to the right of the decimal point, a method called **truncation** is used. This avoids getting an answer such as $5.22211 or 2.1333 hours, which really looks odd.

Here is the method used for truncation:

Take a variable representing an amount and place it into the truncation equation after all the other calculations using that variable in the program have been done.

Here is a step-by-step example using the 2.1333 hours example to show how truncating or rounding 2.1333 to 2.13 takes place.

1. VARIABLE = INT (VARIABLE * 100 +.05) / 100
   This is the complete truncation equation. (Any variable is equal to a whole number, times the variable, times 100, plus .05, divided by 100.)
2. VARIABLE = INT (2.1333 * 100 + .05) / 100 (Assigning the 2.1333 hours example to the variable inside the parentheses.)
3. VARIABLE = INT (213.33 +.05) / 100 (Multiplying by 100 moves the decimal over 2 spaces to the right.)
4. VARIABLE = INT (213.833) / 100 (Adds .05 to the amount.)
5. VARIABLE = 213 (INT cuts off the decimal fraction.)
6. VARIABLE = 2.13 (Dividing by 100 moves the decimal back over 2 spaces to left, giving the final answer, 2.13.)

HERE IS NIBBLES, ROUNDING OFF NUMBERS.

Study a program containing truncation.

Here is a program to study and type with a truncation line to round off an answer before it is printed:

```
NEW
10 HOME
20 REM TIME = DISTANCE DIVIDED BY SPEED
   PROGRAM
25 REM ASSIGN NAMES TO VARIABLES
30 REM TIME = TIME, S = SPEED, DST =
   DISTANCE

35 REM ASSIGN VALUES TO VARIABLES
40 DST = 1448.8
50 S = 5.5
60 TIME = DST / S

65 REM ROUND OFF THE FINAL ANSWER
70 TIME = INT (TIME + .05 * 100) / 100

80 PRINT "IF YOU GO ";DST; " MILES"
90 PRINT "AT "; S; " MILES PER HOUR"
100 PRINT "IT WILL TAKE YOU "; TIME;
    "HOURS."
```

RUN the program; then take out Line 70. (Remember: type 70 and press [RETURN] to erase a line.)

Now RUN the program without the truncation equation.

Now you will see the difference that truncation can make! Make it a part of every program you write that requires calculations. The equation may look a bit complicated at first, but if you understand how the formula works, the procedure will soon be in your own mental memory bank, and you'll be able to write the equation without having to look it up each time. It's worth spending some time now so you'll understand how to use this valuable tool in your future programs.

Relational operators are used to stop GOTO loops.

It is possible to use a GOTO statement to repeat an action. The IF THEN statement, when used with a relational operator, can act as a "brake" to stop a GOTO loop. When the value of the variable has reached the amount following the relational operator by making the desired number of passes or loops, the computer branches to another line of the program.

Study and type the following program:

```
NEW
5  REM COUNTING WITH THE COMPUTER USING IF THEN
10 HOME

20 C = 1                          (Establish a starting point
                                  or value for the variable
                                  C.)

30 PRINT C                        (The variable C = 1. When C
                                  is printed, 1 will appear.)

40 C = C + 1                      (Every time C is printed, 1
                                  will be added to that
                                  number. Now C = 2 because C
                                  = 1 + 1, or 2. Isn't that
                                  clever! It will print up to
                                  10 because the value of C
                                  will change every time there
                                  is a new loop, or pass, up
                                  to Line 30.)

50 IF C = 11 THEN GOTO 70         (If C has enough added on
                                  to equal 11, the program
(The computer compares one        will go to the last line.
more than it prints.)             It wasn't asked to print
                                  11.)

60 GOTO 30                        (If C doesn't equal 11, the
                                  program loops back to Line
                                  30 to print another number.)

70 END
```

Type RUN and press [RETURN] . . . and see the computer count!

Experiment with relational operators used with GOTO loops.

If you want to print all even numbers and count by 2 to 100, change Lines 20, 40, and 50 in the program on the preceding page. Type the following changes:

```
20 C = 2                   (Sets beginning value at 2.)
40 C = C + 2               (Adds 2 each time instead of 1.)

50 IF C => 102 THEN GOTO 70 (If C is equal to or greater than
                           100, the computer ends the loop
                           and branches to Line 70.)
```

If you want to print all odd numbers and still count by 2 up to 99, change lines 20, 40, and 50 in the preceding program.

```
20 C = 1
40 C = C + 2
50 IF C => 100 THEN GOTO 70
```

If you want to count by 5 up to 100, change lines 20, 40, and 50 again.

```
20 C = 5
40 C = C + 5
50 IF C =>105 THEN GOTO 70
```

If you want to go backwards from 100 by 1, change lines 20, 40, and 50 again.

```
20 C = 100
40 C = C - 1
50 IF C =<1 THEN GOTO 70
```

Now experiment using all kinds of numbers with subtraction and addition.

Remember, to stop a Runaway (if your computer gets out of hand and doesn't stop when you want it to as you experiment), press [CONTROL] [C].

Get ready for the BLASTOFF program coming up!

COUNT DOWN TIME!

Blast off using math operators with FOR-NEXT statements.

FOR-NEXT statements can be used with **MATH OPERATORS** and numbers for programs. Have a "blast" doing this program as you study, type, and run it!

Input	Explanation
`NEW`	(Clear the memory.)
`10 REM THIS IS GOING TO BE A BLAST`	(Document the warning!)
`20 HOME`	(Clear the area.)
`30 FOR NUMBER = 10 TO 1 STEP -1`	(NUMBER is the variable which will go from 10 to 1, subtracting 1 each time a loop is made.)
`40 VTAB 12:HTAB 18`	(Front and center, please!)
`50 SPEED = 100`	(Slow things down a bit.)
`60 PRINT NUMBER`	(Start printing with 10.)
`65 FOR TIME = 1 TO 200:NEXT TIME:HOME`	(Clear screen each time a number is printed.)
`70 NEXT NUMBER`	(Keep printing until 1 is reached.)
`80 FOR TIME = 1 TO 200:NEXT TIME` `90 HOME`	(Delay time and clear screen.)
`100 HTAB 15:VTAB 10:INVERSE`	(Center and reverse color.)
`110 PRINT "BLASTOFF"`	(This is it!)
`120 VTAB 24`	(Cursor to bottom of screen.)

READY?

Type NORMAL if you want to list your program. The INVERSE command from Line 100 is great when the program runs, but isn't so great when trying to list and write new lines.

The SPEED command in Line 50 slows the printing of the countdown to make it more effective. When you want to list, however, the slow speed can be a "drag," so change it to SPEED = 255 to return to normal speed.

Computers can add figures together to find totals.

Computers can be used to total various amounts. A total is the sum of two or more numbers. If you want to buy a new outfit, you first must add up the price of each article to know what the total cost will be.

Study and type the following program:

```
NEW
10 HOME
20 REM SUM IS THE TOTAL COST OF SHIRT,
   PANTS, AND TIE
30 SHIRT = 10
40 PANTS = 15
50 TIE = 5
60 SUM = SHIRT + PANTS + TIE
70 PRINT SUM
```

RUN the program.

It will make more sense if the words are printed on the screen as well as the number representing the total. To make this program more user-friendly, add some PRINT statements to the program. LIST and add some more lines to the program.

```
25 VTAB 6:HTAB 13
35 PRINT "CLOTHING EXPENSE"
45 PRINT:PRINT
65 HTAB 16
70 PRINT "SHIRT ";SHIRT
80 HTAB 16
90 PRINT "PANTS " ;PANTS
100 HTAB 16
110 PRINT "TIE    ";TIE (Space four spaces
                       after the first TIE.)
115 HTAB 11
116 PRINT:PRINT
120 PRINT "THE TOTAL COST IS "; SUM
```

IT "ADDS UP" TO A NICE OUTFIT.

(Now RUN the program again and see the difference.)

Now LIST and see the entire program. If you have a printer, type PR #1 and LIST the program in its improved form. Now you know why you should leave increments between line numbers. It is important to be able to add lines and improve programs.

VOCABULARY TO REMEMBER

Basic Commands

SPEED = Command that controls the rate at which a program is listed or executed. The range is from 1 to 255.

Terms

MATH OPERATORS Symbols used in BASIC language to indicate ADDITION +, SUBTRACTION −, MULTIPLICATION *, DIVISION /, and EXPONENTIATION ^.

EXPONENTIATION A number multiplied by itself. The BASIC symbol is similar to a small teepee.

PRECEDENCE Term used in math to indicate the order in which math operators are to be applied.

RELATIONAL OPERATORS Symbols used in BASIC language to make comparisons. EQUAL =, GREATER THAN >, LESS THAN <, NOT EQUAL TO <>.

CONDITIONAL BRANCHING The computer is told to GOTO to a line out of the normal ascending order if a certain condition exists. If the condition does not exist, the usual ascending order is followed.

RESERVED WORD Word which cannot be used as a variable because it is reserved for use as a BASIC command.

TRUNCATION The "rounding off" of an amount to cut off unnecessary places to the right of a decimal.

Creative Corner

Again, it's your turn to demonstrate what you've learned about computers and perhaps about yourself.

This time, write some programs to review what you learned about computer-style math.

1. Write a program that will count by three up to 12. (Hint: use either an IF THEN statement with a GOTO loop or a FOR-NEXT statement.)
2. Write a program that will add four different amounts and total them.
3. Write a program that gives the exponentiation of 4 ^ 3.
4. List the order of precedence of math operators.

Review any pages you need to remind yourself how to do some of these items. Hang in there. Remember your goal is to learn how to use an Apple computer. You are learning more every day!

10
READ DATA AND INPUT STATEMENTS

GOAL: To learn to use READ DATA and INPUT statements in programs.

THOUGHT: Read only the best books, for you become what you read!

Vocabulary To Learn:

BASIC Commands:

READ DATA	INPUT	DIM
PRINT SPC	RND	

TERMS:

DATA TERMINATOR	FILE	ACCUMULATOR
TABLE	RECORD	ARRAY
HEADING	FIELD	SUBSCRIPT
COLUMN HEADING	SUMMARIZE	

READ and DATA must always be used together.

It is efficient to store related items together. For example, socks are folded in pairs and placed with other socks in the same drawer. This saves time in finding them when you need them and saves drawer space too! Related items are stored together in a computer by using READ DATA statements. These two commands must be used together. They are like a pair of socks—one isn't useful without the other!

READ instructs the computer to search through the lines in a program to find the DATA statement and then reads what is written after DATA. The DATA statement contains the information to be stored.

It doesn't matter which line, READ or DATA, comes first or has the lowest line number. READ will go anywhere to find good old DATA. They really are inseparable! However, DATA is usually listed at the very end of a program to make it easier to add new information or make changes in the DATA line.

WHERE ELSE CAN A WORM WEAR SOMETHING THIS INSEPARABLE?

Phone lists can be made using READ DATA.

A list of friends and their phone numbers can be written using a READ DATA program. Here's a sample of two names and phone numbers written after a DATA command.

```
DATA "LISA", "944-3333", "DEAN", "333-4747"
```

Quotes may be placed around each data item but they are not necessary. The commas separating the items are essential. The computer uses these symbols to know where each item begins and ends.

READ must have a variable or variables written after it.

```
READ NAME$, NUMBER$
DATA "LISA", "944-3333", "DEAN", "333-4747"
```

The variables NAME$ and NUMBER$ will be assigned to the actual names and numbers following DATA, according to the order in which they are listed. The computer doesn't know that "NAME" means a person's name or "NUMBER" means the phone number. However, it makes it easier to use variables that people can understand, even if the computer can't.

The computer reads according to the order of items listed after DATA. The first item after DATA will be the first one the computer will read. This item will then be assigned to the first variable listed after READ. So "LISA" will be read first and assigned to NAME$; and "944-3333" will be read next and assigned to NUMBER$. The next time DATA is read, after a GOTO loop, "DEAN" will be read and assigned to NAME$; and "333-4747" will be read and assigned to NUMBER$. The computer remembers where it left off in the DATA list when it comes back to read the next item.

The PRINT statement must be used with READ DATA.

The PRINT statement must be used to PRINT the characters listed after DATA. The same variables that were used with the READ statement must follow the PRINT statement.

Study and type the following:

```
NEW
5 HOME
10 READ NAME$, NUMBER$
20 PRINT NAME$, NUMBER$
30 DATA "LISA", "944-3333", "DEAN", "333-4747"
```

This will print only "LISA" and her number. To be able to read and print both "LISA" and "DEAN," there must be a loop back to the READ statement in Line 10, so that it can be READ again. Here is an example to study and type:

```
NEW
10 HOME
20 READ NAME$, NUMBER$
30 PRINT NAME$, NUMBER$
40 GOTO 20
50 DATA "LISA", "944-3333", "DEAN", "333-4747"
60 END
```

The computer will first READ and PRINT "LISA" and her phone number, then GOTO line 20 and READ and PRINT "DEAN" and his number.

If READ cannot find DATA because no DATA line was written, or if there is nothing else to read after "DEAN","333-4747", an OUT OF DATA ERROR will appear on the screen. To avoid this, **data terminators** are used to indicate the end of data. Dummy data is another term used for the ending information after a DATA line. It is called dummy data because it isn't real data; for example, 000,000,000 obviously isn't real data. Just think of store dummies, or mannequins; they aren't real people but they can be used to display clothes, etc., just as dummy data can be used to represent the end of a data list.

HELP STAMP OUT "OUT OF DATA" ERRORS.

IF THEN is used with DATA terminators.

An IF THEN command must be used in a READ DATA program to avoid having an OUT OF DATA error. The computer must compare items written after DATA to see if they match the last items or dummy data characters. If there is a match of characters, the computer will be instructed to GOTO another line and stop the loop between READ and DATA. EOD, which stands for End of Data, is frequently used as dummy data.

```
IF NAME$ ="EOD" THEN GOTO 100
```

Here is a program that will print a phone list using the READ DATA command with an EOD. Study and type the following:

Input	Explanation
`NEW`	
`10 HOME`	
`20 VTAB 6:HTAB 15`	(Centers the heading.)
`30 PRINT "PHONE LIST"`	(Heading.)
`40 READ NAME$, NUMBER$`	
`50 PRINT:PRINT`	(Leaves 2 spaces.)
`60 HTAB 7`	(Spaces over 7 from left.)
`70 IF NAME$ = "EOD " THEN GOTO 100`	(Compares.)
`80 PRINT NAME$, NUMBER$`	(Prints names and numbers.)
`90 GOTO 40`	(Loops back to 40.)
`100 DATA "LISA", "944-5888","DEAN", "366-8888", "MARJORIE","444-3333", "EOD", "000"`	
`110 END`	

RUN the program.

To list names and numbers of people you know, just retype Line 100 and change the DATA. For example: (100 DATA "SUE", "449-4444", "RODNEY", "944-5555", "SALLY", "955-8765", "EOD", "000")

Study and type a READ DATA phone list program

Input	Explanation
NEW	(Clears memory.)
10 HOME	(Clears screen.)
20 VTAB 6:HTAB 15	(Spaces 6 down from the top line and 15 from the left margin.)
30 PRINT "PHONE LIST"	(This is the title.)
40 READ NAME$, NUMBER$	(READ will search for DATA and assign the amounts in DATA to the variables.)
50 PRINT:PRINT	(Leaves two blank spaces after the title.)
60 HTAB 7	(Spaces over 7 from left.)
70 IF NAME$ = "EOD" THEN GOTO 110	(The computer will compare the string variable to see if it matches EOD. If it does, the computer will branch to 110; if it doesn't, the computer will continue to Line 80.)
80 PRINT NAME$, NUMBER$	(The computer will print the names and numbers from DATA in two columns because of the commas between the two string variables.)
90 GOTO 40	(Instructed to return to Line 40 where it will be told to READ another entry listed under DATA.)
100 DATA "LISA", "944-5888", "DEAN", "366-8888", "MARJORIE", "444-3333", "EOD", "000"	(The data items are separated by commas to let the computer know beginnings and endings. Quotes make it easier for people to separate the items, but they are not necessary.)
110 END	

Learn to make a table.

A **table** is used to list related items together. At the beginning of a table is a **heading** or title. Next, a subheading may follow, giving additional information about the title or subject. A table is usually divided into separate rows, each with a descriptive **column heading**.

Here is an example:

```
             MY ADDRESS AND TELEPHONE LIST

              Property of Lisa Ann Bennett

  Name                    Address                   Phone Number

Stacey Baxter  4449 W. Orange Drive, Phx Az     939-6049
Sally Jones    128 State Ave, Phx Az            944-5858
Bob Smith      453 West Orange, Phx Az          934-5121
Sue Single     213 South Dunlap, Phx AZ         954-3330
```

The main heading is "MY ADDRESS AND TELEPHONE LIST." The subheading is "Property of Lisa Ann Bennett." The column headings are "Name," "Address," and "Phone Number." The actual names, addresses, and phone numbers are called the body of the TABLE.

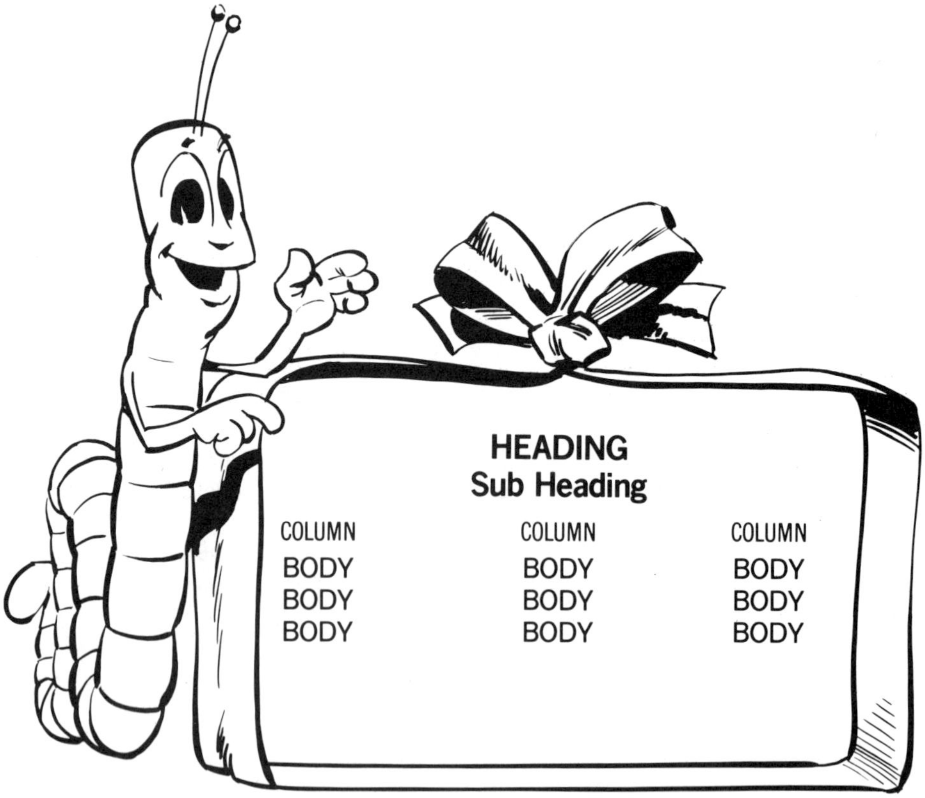

A TABLE IS A NEAT WAY TO KEEP THINGS IN ORDER.

Files, Records, and Fields are used in programming.

File is the computer term given to identify related information such as a table or phone list. A **field** is one of the columns of information. In the example above: Name is the first field, Address is the second, and Phone Number is the third. A **record** is a group of fields. A name, address, and phone number from the phone list would make up a record.

Learn more about the PRINT TAB statement.

Remember, the PRINT TAB command can be used to space columns. TAB cannot be used by itself; it must be used with PRINT. The desired horizontal column on the screen, counting from the left margin, is placed in parentheses following TAB. For example:

```
40 PRINT TAB (4);"HELLO"
```

would print "HELLO" in the fourth horizontal column.

```
50 PRINT TAB (10) "AGAIN"
```

would print "AGAIN" in the tenth horizontal column.

The amount in parentheses indicates the exact column number; it does not give the number of spaces to tabulate or "move over." The amount in parentheses may be a number (constant), a variable, or an arithmetic expression such as 3 + 2. Study and type the following program:

```
NEW
10 HOME
20 REM USING PRINT TAB FOR COLUMNS
30 PRINT TAB (5); "HELLO"         (Constant 5 used with TAB.)
40 X = 5                          (Assign value to X.)
50 PRINT TAB (X); "HELLO"         (Variable used with TAB.)
60 PRINT TAB (3 + 2); "HELLO"     (Expression used with TAB.)
```

It is usually advisable to use a variable following PRINT TAB because the number assigned to the variable can be easily changed.

More than one TAB may be listed after the same PRINT in a statement. When there is more than one TAB, semicolons MUST be used to separate the TAB and its parentheses from the other items in the statement. Each TAB must move the cursor FORWARD when there are several TAB commands following PRINT.

Use spacing charts to know how to arrange copy.

Before writing a phone list or similar type program, you should first use a spacing chart to know exactly how many spaces to leave between columns, etc. Graph paper can be used; however, computer spacing sheets are easier to use because of the printed numbers on the chart. If a printer is going to be used, the spacing chart should indicate an 80-space line. Usually about 65 spaces are used out of the 80 spaces on a printer to allow for margins. The monitor screen has 40 spaces. This program is written for the monitor screen. Study the following; then type it.

```
NEW
10 HOME
20 VTAB 4
30 PRINT TAB(5); "MY ADDRESS AND TELEPHONE
   LIST"
40 VTAB 6
50 PRINT TAB (6); "PROPERTY OF LISA ANN
   BENNETT"
60 VTAB 10
70 PRINT TAB (1); "NAME";
   TAB(15);"ADDRESS";
   TAB (29);"PHONE NUMBER"

80 VTAB 12
90 READ NAME$, ADDRESS$, NUMBER$
100 IF NAME$ ="EOD" THEN GO TO 130
110 PRINT TAB(1); NAME$; TAB(12);
    ADDRESS$; TAB(30); NUMBER$
120 GOTO 90
130 END
200 DATA SALLY, 444 STATE AVE, 944-3333,
    DEAN, 432 S. STATE, 432-5858
250 DATA MARJORIE, 333 S. OLIVE, 444-3333,
    "EOD","000","000","000"
```

Change the spacing in Lines 30, 50, 70, and 110 to allow for more spacing after the TAB commands if using a printer. Also change VTAB commands, which don't work on a printer, to PRINT commands for vertical spacing. Add lines to activate the printer.

```
15 PR#1         (This will turn on the printer)
120 GOTO 140 (Turn off the printer before going
                to END.)
140 PR#0        (This will turn off the printer.)
```

Learn to use the SPC (space) command.

The SPC command is used to indicate the exact number of spaces to "space" over to the right before printing characters. With SPC, the computer doesn't consider the number of the horizontal column; it counts over the actual number of spaces from the last position of the cursor.

SPC is used in much the same manner as the PRINT TAB; it must always be used with PRINT. It must be separated from other items with semicolons when more than one SPC is used with a PRINT statement.

```
30 PRINT SPC (15); "HI THERE!"
```

SPC may be used with variables to indicate the number of spaces to tabulate.

```
15 X = 5
30 PRINT SPC (X); "HI THERE!"
40 PRINT SPC (X); "HI THERE!"; SPC(X);"HI
   AGAIN!"
```

The computer will space over 5 spaces before printing "HI THERE!" and then space over 5 more before printing "HI AGAIN!"

The printer treats PRINT TAB as if it were PRINT SPC. It moves printing over the exact number and doesn't consider the number of the horizontal column.

NIBBLES CALLING "SPC COMMAND."

People enjoy seeing their names on the screen.

Printing a person's name on the screen—whether it's a game or an educational program makes it seem much friendlier. It's fun to see your name in lights! That makes anyone feel extra special! Anyone's name can be put into a program by using an INPUT statement. With an INPUT statement, the person at the keyboard can interact and add information, such as a name, to the program.

IT'S FUN TO SEE YOUR NAME IN LIGHTS.

The INPUT command is used with variables and string variables. The INPUT reserves areas in memory for names, or any information, coming into the program after the program was first written.

Study and type the following:

```
NEW
5 HOME
10 PRINT "WHAT IS YOUR NAME? "
20 INPUT NAME$
30 PRINT "YOU ARE BECOMING AN EXPERT,
   ";NAME$
```

RUN the program. Type in your name when asked by the computer.

Line 10 is a PRINT statement asking someone to type in information that wasn't known when the program was written. Line 20 reserves space in memory for NAME$. The string variable will be replaced by the name entered from the keyboard.

Line 30 will print the message and then print the person's name. Notice there are no quotes around NAME$. Everyone would be called NAME$ if quotes were placed around the variable.

Do you want to know how old someone is?

If the "new" information coming in from the keyboard INPUT statement contains only numbers, a variable may be used, leaving off the string ($). Study and type this "masterpiece." (By the way, don't run this program for an "older" lady! She may not like it.)

```
NEW
10 HOME
20 PRINT "HOW OLD ARE YOU?"
30 INPUT AGE
40 PRINT "ARE YOU REALLY "; AGE ;"?"
```

Type RUN, and answer the questions as they appear on the screen.

Notice that the variable is set off from the literal by a semicolon. Remember, the literal is the section set off by quotes. Even the question mark has to be set off by quotes to print it at the end of the sentence.

Leave a space following the word "REALLY", so that the new information has a space before it.

Example: ARE YOU REALLY ";AGE ;"?" Otherwise, the output would look like this: ARE YOU REALLY16?

PRINT and INPUT may be put together into one statement.

Study line 20 in the following:

```
20 INPUT "WHAT IS YOUR NAME ?"; NAME$
30 PRINT " HI, " ; NAME$; "LET'S BE FRIENDS"
```

The PRINT is "understood" when it is replaced by INPUT. Don't use both PRINT and INPUT in the same statement. It won't work! The computer gets "indigestion" from too many instructions! The literal in quotes will be printed exactly as it is written. The semicolon separates the string variable from the literal. The results are the same as they would be if PRINT and INPUT were written separately.

Enjoy using INPUT.

You can have a lot of fun using the INPUT statement. Here are some sample questions to ask yourself . . . and someone else.

Study and type the following:

```
NEW
5 REM FRIENDLY QUESTIONS
10 HOME
20 INPUT "WHERE DO YOU LIVE? "; CITY$
30 PRINT CITY$ ; " IS A NICE TOWN."
40 INPUT "WHAT IS YOUR FAVORITE FOOD? ";
   FOOD$
50 PRINT FOOD$; " IS ONE OF MY FAVORITES,
   TOO!"
60 INPUT "TELL ME YOUR NAME SO I'LL
   REMEMBER. ";NAME$
70 PRINT NAME$ "; IS A WINNER!"
```

To make it even more interesting, IF THEN can be used with INPUT statements to make comparisons and branching. Study and type the following:

```
NEW
5 REM MORE FRIENDLY QUESTIONS WITH INPUT
10 HOME

20 INPUT "TYPE THE NUMBER OF YOUR FAVORITE
   PAST TIME."
30 PRINT "1) SPORTS  2) READING  3) TV "

40 INPUT A
50 IF A = 1 THEN PRINT "SPORTS ARE GREAT."
60 IF A = 2 THEN PRINT "GOOD CHOICE."
70 IF A = 3 THEN PRINT "BE SELECTIVE!"

80 PRINT "THANKS FOR YOUR TIME."
90 PRINT "IT'S FUN TO GET ACQUAINTED!"
100 END
```

RUN the program and answer the question.

Now make up some of your own INPUT statements. Use some IF THEN comparisons to branch to other lines. You can do many things using these commands.

NOW YOU AND YOUR COMPUTER ARE ON FRIENDLY TERMS.

Prompts let a user know what to do next.

It is necessary to use a prompt to let the person at the keyboard know what to answer. If there is no PRINT statement used with INPUT, only a question mark will appear, and that's confusing. (Things like this are what give computers a bad name!) Study the following:

```
NEW
10 HOME
20 INPUT A
```

RUN the program.

(Nothing appears but a confusing question mark.) Press [CONTROL] [RESET] to stop the program and get rid of the silly question mark. Press [CONTROL] [RESET] again to stop the disk drive from booting. Now change Line 20 so that it makes sense.

```
20 INPUT "DO YOU LIKE WORKING ON A
   COMPUTER? Y/N ";A$
30 IF A$ = "Y" THEN PRINT "WAY TO GO!
   THAT'S GREAT!"
40 IF A$ = "N" THEN PRINT "DON'T GIVE UP!
   YOU CAN DO IT!"
```

Run the program and answer the questions on the screen.

Notice that with string variables in Lines 30 and 40, quotes must be placed around the answers. With numeric variables, no quotes are necessary. Here's an example of variables with no quotes:

```
NEW
10 HOME
20 PRINT "HOW MUCH DO YOU WEIGH?"
30 PRINT "SHH I WON'T TELL! "
40 INPUT WEIGHT
50 IF WEIGHT < 100 THEN PRINT "YOU MUST BE
   PETITE!"
60 IF WEIGHT > 100 THEN PRINT "YOU MUST BE
   GROWN UP!"
70 END
```

(In Line 50, the comparison is made between 100 and the amount assigned to the variable WEIGHT. If the amount is smaller than 100, then the message in Line 50 is printed. If WEIGHT is greater than 100, then the message in Line 60 is printed.)

The RANDOM (RND) statement can be fun to use too!

The INPUT is often used with a random statement which is indicated in BASIC as RND.

Random (RND) means without any certain order. Closing your eyes and picking a winner's name from a box would be selecting at random. The only limit placed on your random choice would be the number of names that were in the box.

This is an example of the Apple random function: (You can stop this runaway by pressing [CONTROL] [C].)

```
NEW
5 HOME
8 REM LEARNING ABOUT RANDOM NUMBERS
10 PRINT RND (1)
20 GOTO 10
```

RUN the program.

The RND in Line 10 stands for random. The RND function produces a different sample of numbers each time you run it.

The numbers produced by this program are random decimal fractions between zero and one.

Use INT to round off decimals.

To get rid of the clumsy decimal fractions, the Integer (**INT**) command is used with RND. This rounds off the decimals to the nearest integer number. Press [CONTROL] [C] to stop the program.

Study and type the following:

```
NEW
10 REM ASSIGN RANDOM NUMBERS TO THE
   VARIABLE X
20 X = RND(1)

30 REM MULTIPLY X BY 10
40 X = X * 10

50 REM ROUND OFF THE FRACTIONS
60 X = INT(X)
70 PRINT X
80 GOTO 100
```

To change the program so that it prints numbers from 1 to 10 instead of from 0 to 9, add this line to the program:

65 X = X + 1

Run the program to see what happens.

Study this step-by-step explanation of a RND program.

The RND may seem a bit complicated until you get used to working with it. To let you see what happens step by step, study this program, even if it doesn't make much sense as you type it. When you see the program as it runs, you'll understand it more—I promise! The speed is slowed down so you'll have a chance to study each line. Use [CONTROL] [C], not [CONTROL] [RESET] when you want to stop the program. You'll lose your program if you use [CONTROL] [RESET], and have to retype it. Save it on a disk for future reference so you won't have to retype it when you want to study it again. Type carefully.

```
NEW
10  HOME
15  SPEED = 75
20  INVERSE:VTAB 10:HTAB 8
30  PRINT "PRESENTING RANDOM...RND"
40  NORMAL
50  FOR TIME = 1 TO 2000:NEXT TIME
60  HOME
70  PRINT "THESE ARE THE STEPS FOR
    SELECTING RND"
80  PRINT "NUMBERS FROM 1 TO 10:"
85  PRINT
90  PRINT "ASSIGN RND NUMBER TO X"
100 PRINT
```

```
110 X = RND (1):PRINT "X = RND(1)",X
120 PRINT
130 PRINT "MULTIPLY BY 10 TO MOVE DECIMAL"
140 X = X * 10:PRINT
150 PRINT "X = X * 10";X
160 PRINT
170 PRINT "ROUND OFF THE FRACTION":PRINT
180 X = INT (X):PRINT "X = INT(X)",X
190 PRINT
200 PRINT "ADD 1 TO THE VALUE OF X":PRINT
210 X = X + 1:PRINT "X = X + 1",X
220 PRINT:PRINT
230 PRINT "THIS RANDOM NUMBER IS ";
240 PRINT X
250 FOR TIME = 1 TO 2000:NEXT TIME
260 HOME
270 GOTO 90
```

Run the program and see the RND do "its thing!"

Have some rest and relaxation with a RND game.

Phew . . . you need a rest after that long random program. Here is a game to play using INPUT with a shortened RND command. (Notice Line 90.) This game is called "GUESS THE NUMBER."

Type in and play the following:

```
NEW
10 HOME
20 REM GUESS THE NUMBER GAME
30 REM ATTRACTIVELY ARRANGE AND PRINT THE
   TITLE
40 VTAB 10: HTAB 12
50 PRINT "GUESS THE NUMBER"

60 REM SET A TIME LOOP AND CLEAR THE
   SCREEN
70 FOR X = 1 TO 2000:NEXT X:HOME

80 REM SET THE RND LIMITS FOR A NUMBER
   BETWEEN 1 AND 10
90 NUMBER = INT(RND (1) * 10) +1

100 PRINT "GUESS THE NUMBER THE COMPUTER
    IS THINKING"
110 PRINT "BETWEEN ONE AND TEN"
120 PRINT:PRINT
125 REM GUESS IS THE NUMBER CHOSEN BY THE
    PLAYER.
128 REM NUMBER IS THE NUMBER CHOSEN BY THE
    COMPUTER.
130 INPUT GUESS
```

```
140 REM MAKE A BRANCH TO THE END IF THE
    ANSWER IS CORRECT.
150 IF NUMBER = GUESS THEN PRINT
    "CORRECT":GOTO 310

160 REM MAKE A BRANCH FOR ANSWER THAT'S
    TOO HIGH
170 IF NUMBER < GUESS THEN PRINT "GUESS
    LOWER, TRY AGAIN":GOTO 100

180 REM MAKE A BRANCH FOR ANSWER THAT'S
    TOO LOW
190 IF NUMBER > GUESS THEN PRINT "GUESS
    HIGHER, TRY AGAIN":GOTO 100

300 REM PRINT THANKS FOR PLAYING AND
    COMPLIMENT THE WINNER.
310 PRINT "THANKS FOR PLAYING!"
320 PRINT "YOU ARE GOOD AT GUESSING!"
330 END
```

WIN SOME, LOSE SOME.

Practice multiplication using RND statements.

Here's a program to study and type using random with INPUT to help someone learn to multiply by 12s.

```
NEW
10 REM LEARNING THE TIMES TABLES
20 HOME
```

```
30 REM GET ACQUAINTED. LEARN NAME. NAME$ =
   PLAYER'S NAME
40 INPUT "WHAT IS YOUR NAME? ";NAME$
50 PRINT:PRINT
60 PRINT "HERE ARE THE TIMES TABLES FOR
   12, ";NAME$

70 REM SET THE VARIABLE C AT ZERO TO BE
   READY TO COUNT
80 C = 0

90 REM ASSIGN 12 TO THE VARIABLE A1
100 A1 = 12
110 REM FIX SPEED SO PROGRAM WILL PRINT
    SLOWLY
120 SPEED = 100

130 REM ASSIGN RANDOM NUMBERS FROM 1 TO 12
    TO THE VARIABLE A2
140 A2 = INT (RND (1) * 12)

150 REM START THE COUNTER TO ALLOW FOR 3
    PROBLEMS
160 C = C+1

170 REM ASSIGN VARIABLE B TO REPRESENT THE
    ANSWERS
180 B = A1 * A2
190 PRINT:PRINT

200 REM PREPARE TO DISPLAY THE PROBLEMS
    AND ANSWERS
210 HTAB 10
220 PRINT A1 "TIMES " A2 " EQUALS " ;B
230 PRINT:PRINT

240 REM PREPARE TO BRANCH AFTER 3 PROBLEMS
250 IF C = 3 THEN GOTO 290

260 REM PREPARE TO LOOP FOR LESS THAN 3
    PROBLEMS
270 GOTO 140

280 REM ASK IF PLAYER WANTS TO DO MORE
    PROBLEMS
290 INPUT "DO YOU WISH TO SEE MORE? Y/N
    ";A$
300 REM PREPARE BRANCH FOR DECISION
310 IF A$ = "Y" THEN GOTO 140
320 IF A$ = "N" THEN GOTO 330
330 HOME: PRINT "THANKS FOR PLAYING, ";
    NAME$
340 END
```

*If you wish to multiply by a number other than 12, assign a new amount to the variable A1 in Line 100.

Learn to use an accumulator to summarize.

Adding several numbers and printing their totals is called **summarizing**, useful for adding items such as expenses, school credits, etc.

A variable which is used for storing various amounts as they are being gathered is sometimes called an **accumulator**. The first step is to assign zero to the accumulator; then it will be added to every amount as it is read. By the time the entire list has been read, the accumulator will have the grand total.

Study and type the following:

```
NEW
10 HOME
20 SUM = 0                        (The ACCUMULATOR is set at 0.)

30 READ AMOUNT                    (The first DATA item will be
                                  read.)

40 IF AMOUNT <=0 THEN GO TO 80    (If the amount is the terminator,
                                  zero, the computer is told to
                                  print the total.

50 PRINT AMOUNT                   (The amount listed under DATA is
                                  printed.)

60 SUM = SUM + AMOUNT             (The variable SUM is added to the
                                  first amount.)

70 GOTO 30                        (The computer is told to loop to
                                  Line 30.)

80 PRINT SUM ; "SUM"              (The SUM will now be printed.)

90 END                            (The end of the show!)

100 DATA 3, 5, 10, 0              (These amounts will be read and
                                  printed.)
```

Type RUN and give this one a workout!

Change the figures under DATA to experiment with adding other amounts.

Average a group of numbers.

To find the average of a group of numbers, they first must be added together with an accumulator, then divided by their total number. Using numbers to indicate letter grades, (1 = A, 2 = B, 3 = C, 4 = D, and 5 = F), enter in your grades and find the average.

Study and type the following:

```
NEW
10 HOME
20 SUM = 0
30 INPUT "HOW MANY GRADES ARE YOU GOING TO
   ENTER? ";N
40 FOR X = 1 TO N
50 INPUT "ENTER YOUR GRADES ";N1
60 SUM = SUM + N1
70 NEXT X
80 SUM = SUM / N
90 SUM = INT (SUM * 100 + .5) / 100
100 PRINT "YOUR GRADE AVERAGE IS ";SUM
120 END
```

MY GRADES WOULD BE BETTER IF THE TEACHER WOULD USE MY PROGRAM.

You are asked to give the number of grades to be averaged. Your answer is assigned to the variable N. The number of loops made will be "based" on the amount of N. The FOR-NEXT loop will be written: FOR X = 1 TO N, because N represents the unknown number of grades entered from the keyboard. If you want to average 5 grades, the variable will be N = 5. The loop will go from 1 to 5 times or FOR X = 1 TO 5. If you enter 8 as your request, then 8 will be assigned to N; and the loop will go from 1 to 8 times.

The grades are all INPUT to the variable N1. The variable, SUM, accumulates the grades as they are entered from the keyboard (SUM = SUM + N1). After the loop has been completed, the variable SUM is divided by N, the number of grades that were added. Then SUM is truncated to round off "excess baggage" decimal places. It's the big numbers on the left side of the decimal that count!

Related numbers in a table can be assigned to the same variable.

Related numbers in a table can share the same variable; this is called an **array**. If you are figuring your expenses for the month and have several similar items for clothing, food, car expense, etc., it is convenient to classify them together as a group, or an array, so they can be rearranged and calculated. Here's an example: Suppose on one day you bought a book that cost $20; another day you bought one for $10; and another day, you couldn't resist one for $25! For convenience, these can be placed in one array, all using the same variable when figuring money spent for books.

The variable could be called BOOK. The assigned value would be the cost of the BOOK. The first purchase could be called BOOK 1 and would be assigned 20; the second could be called BOOK 2 and be assigned 10; the third would be called BOOK 3 and be assigned 25.

The name of the array is BOOK. It has three subdivisions:

VARIABLE NAME	ASSIGNED VALUE
BOOK (1)	20
BOOK (2)	10
BOOK (3)	25

The numbers in parentheses designate the subdivisions; they are called **subscripts**. In computer jargon, this is shortened to Sub. So the first book is called BOOK Sub 1; the second BOOK, Sub 2, etc. The subscript helps a person locate the exact item. Subscripts can be rearranged and calculated in many ways.

Dimension statements reserve space for arrays.

When a program has one or more arrays, the computer must know how big each array will be to reserve a spot in memory. It's like having enough places set for dinner when you're having guests. You must have enough places set for your guests to make it possible to serve them!

On a computer, you reserve spots in memory by using a dimension statement (DIM). For example, you have three books you've purchased; now add other items to your expenses for some other arrays.

Buy three records, besides the three books . . . why not live it up! The records cost \$9, \$5, and \$10. Assign them to a variable RCD. You can't use RECORD because part of it is a reserved word.

So the records would be RCD (1) = 9 (This is what they cost.)
RCD (2) = 5
RCD (3) = 10

Remember the books were BOOK (1) = 20 (This is what
BOOK (2) = 10 they cost.)
BOOK (3) = 25

Here is the dimension (DIM) statement for these arrays:

```
10 DIM RCD (3), BOOK (3)
```

The DIM indicates that RCD and BOOK have three sections or arrays. When the computer reads this dimension statement, it will set aside six storage slots in its memory banks for these items.

Place DIM at the first of a program.

The dimension (DIM) statement can be placed anywhere in a program, but it is preferred to put DIM near the top of the program to make sure it gets put in before the arrays are listed. In this way, the arrays will have their "seats" reserved for them before they enter. Study and type the following program:

```
NEW
10 HOME
15 REM EXPENSES FOR RECORDS AND BOOKS
20 DIM RCD(3), BOOK (3)
30 READ RCD(1), RCD(2), RCD(3), BOOK(1),
   BOOK(2), BOOK(3)
40 IF RCD(1) = 0 THEN GOTO 100
50 PRINT TAB(1);"RECORDS COST";TAB(15);
   RCD(1);TAB(20);RCD(2); TAB((28);RCD(3)
60 PRINT TAB (1);"BOOKS COST"; TAB(15);
   BOOK(1);TAB(20);BOOK(2); TAB (28); BOOK (3)
70 T = RCD(1) + RCD(2) + RCD(3) + BOOK(1) +
```

```
    BOOK(2) + BOOK(3)
80 PRINT "THE TOTAL COST OF EXPENSE WAS "; T
100 END
200 DATA 9, 5, 10, 20, 10, 25, 0
```

Line 20 dimensions the RCD and BOOK variables so they'll have 3 slots each reserved in memory. Line 30 reads all of the DATA items in order and assigns the record and book arrays with the figures listed in order. RCD (1) would be assigned 9; RCD (2) would be assigned 5, and so on. Line 40 compares to see if all the DATA has been read. The data terminator is 0. If all is finished, the computer "meekly" ends the loop and goes to Line 100.

Line 50 prints the record arrays with the title RECORDS COST. Notice the nifty use of PRINT TAB! It really does a nice job. Line 60 prints the BOOK arrays with its title. Line 70 adds up everything using the T variable as an accumulator. Line 80 prints out so you can see the total. Line 100 is the end of the program, and Line 200 lists the DATA.

VOCABULARY TO REMEMBER

BASIC Commands

READ DATA Statements always used together to input information into a BASIC program. The READ command instructs the computer to find the nearest DATA statement to collect the values listed after DATA, to assign to the variables listed after READ.

PRINT SPC Commands which are similar to PRINT TAB except that the amount in parentheses following SPC indicates the exact number of blank spaces to be printed before printing characters.

INPUT A statement used to input data obtained from a computer user into a BASIC program. The INPUT command places a question mark on the screen and reserves room in memory for the user's reply. An explanation prompt should be added to INPUT to instruct the user what information is desired. The user's response is assigned to a variable.

RND Command which produces numbers in an unstructured random order, which can be used for games and computer assisted instruction application programs.

DIM Command which reserves storage slots in the computer memory bank for an array.

Terms

DATA TERMINATOR The last item listed in a DATA statement which can be used to avoid an OUT OF DATA error when used with an IF THEN statement.

TABLE An organized collection of information that contains a heading and columns.

HEADING The title or first line of a table.

COLUMN HEADING The first line, or title, of a column that describes the information found in that column.

FILE A collection of information stored as a unit, such as a table.

FIELD A section of a file, such as a column from a table.

RECORD A group of fields relating to the same subject, such as the name, address, and phone number of one person from a list.

SUMMARIZE Adding or totaling figures together to obtain large-scale information, such as total yearly income and expenses, grade averages, etc.

ACCUMULATOR A variable that is used to store and total more than one amount, such as collecting and storing a list of purchases or expenses to find the total amount.

ARRAY A table that contains related data that can be calculated and rearranged. A variable is assigned to represent the array. The variable is divided into subdivisions, called subcripts to represent various items or sections.

SUBSCRIPT A section of an array or table that is called Sub for short. Subscripts are used for sorting within an array.

Creative Corner

Here are some exercises to help you know what you've learned:

1. What will be assigned to the variables in these lines?

```
40 READ A$,A
50 DATA "SALLY", "2"
```

2. What will be assigned to the variables in these lines?

```
40 READ A,"A$"
50 DATA 4, "PETE"
```

3. What will be assigned to the variables in these lines?

```
40 READ A$,A
50 END
60 DATA "PETE", "45", "STEVE", "33"
```

4. What will be the output for these lines?

```
NEW
40 READ A$,A
50 IF A$ ="EOD" THEN GOTO 70
55 ?A$, A
60 GOTO 40
70 END
80 DATA "PETE", "45", "STEVE", "33", "EOD", "00"
```

5. What will be assigned to the variables in these lines?

```
40 PRINT "WHAT IS YOUR NAME?"
50 INPUT NAME$
```

(Psst . . . the answers follow!)

ANSWERS TO CREATIVE CORNER

1. A$ will be assigned “SALLY”, and A will be assigned 2.
2. A will be assigned 2, and A$ will be assigned “PETE”.
3. Only “PETE” will be assigned to A$ and 45 to A because the computer doesn't loop back to line 40 to read again.
4.
```
PETE     45
STEVE    33
OUT OF DATA IN LINE 40 (because there is no EOD)

PETE     45
STEVE    33 (EOD will not be printed. It is a DATA TER-
            MINATOR.)
```
5. The user's name will be assigned to NAME$.

Did you know most of these? Go back and reread if you need to make certain you understand READ DATA and INPUT. You'll be using these commands a great deal.

11
THE PORTABLE APPLE IIc

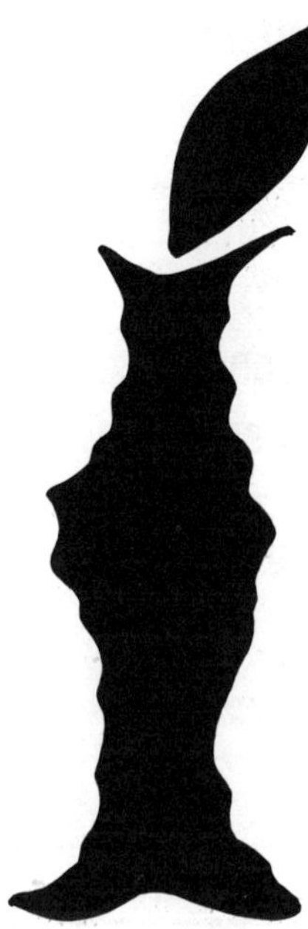

GOAL: To become acquainted with the portable Apple IIc computer.

THOUGHT: Love that is whispered is more powerful than anger that is shouted.

Aa Bb Cc Dd Ee Ff Gg Hh Ii Jj Kk Ll Mm

Vocabulary To Learn:

TERMS:

ICON	LOGO	TELECOMMUNICATIONS
PORTAL	ProDOS	INTEGRATED SOFTWARE
MODEM	PASCAL	DATA BASE
SPREADSHEET	SYSTEM UTILITIES DISK	LIQUID CRYSTAL MONITOR

The Apple IIc differs from the other Apple II family members.

The Apple IIc differs enough from the other members of the Apple II family to deserve its own chapter. The Apple IIc was designed before the Apple IIe, but it took time for the necessary technology to be developed before the IIc could be built and put on the market. The IIe was an improvement over the earlier Apple II and II Plus, adding more memory, upper and lower case, the open apple key for starting up a disk, etc., but it doesn't look very different from the other models.

The IIc is a dramatic change from the rest of the Apple II family. But one of the nicest things about the Apple IIc is its compatibility with the other Apple computers. It can use most of the outstanding selection of software already made for the Apple II series.

THEY'RE ALL IN THE SAME FAMILY, BUT EACH IS DIFFERENT FROM THE REST—JUST LIKE THE APPLE II FAMILY.

Here are some of the differences of the IIc.

The Apple IIc differs noticeably from the rest of the Apple II family in size and general appearance. In a classroom containing Apple II, II Plus, and IIe models, it is difficult to tell one model from another at a distance. But with the IIc, there is no question—it stands out from the others.

THE IIc CAN GO ANYWHERE!

The Apple IIc was designed to be more portable than the earlier models. It weighs less and has a trimmer, more compact appearance. The built-in disk drive is convenient, making one less piece of equipment to carry. The IIc has a light, almost white color. The other Apple II models are beige. The keyboard on the IIc appears to be smaller because it has less area surrounding the keys than the other Apples. The actual area for the hands is the same, however. It is a full-sized keyboard. The IIc computer has a flat appearance until it is propped up by the carrying handle which elevates the the back of the computer and slants the keyboard. This creates a better angle for typing and allows air to circulate underneath the computer. The handle is also used for carrying the computer.

Even the Apple trademark logo is smaller on the IIc. It is located inconspicuously in the upper left corner and appears without the usual Apple printed name. It just has IIc to identify it.

The power light on the IIc is a slender indicator located above the keyboard on the right, next to the disk drive indicator. The power indicator on the other Apple II models is located to the left of the space bar on the keyboard.

The Apple IIc is easy to assemble.

A picture or illustration can be a helpful teacher. The Apple IIc has small engraved pictures called **icons** that indicate the correct places to plug in peripheral equipment. These little pictures are located at the back of the computer above six openings called **portals**. Cords and cables are inserted into these openings and joined to circuitry inside the computer. The icons help remind a person to use the correct portal, regardless of the language the person speaks.

The **portals** are as follows:

1. The mouse or game joystick.
2. The **modem**.
3. The television adaptor switch box.
4. The computer monitor.
5. The additional disk drive. It has an icon of a disk.
6. The printer.
7. The power supply connector into which is plugged either the power supply or the battery pack. (Refer to your instruction booklet for further information.)

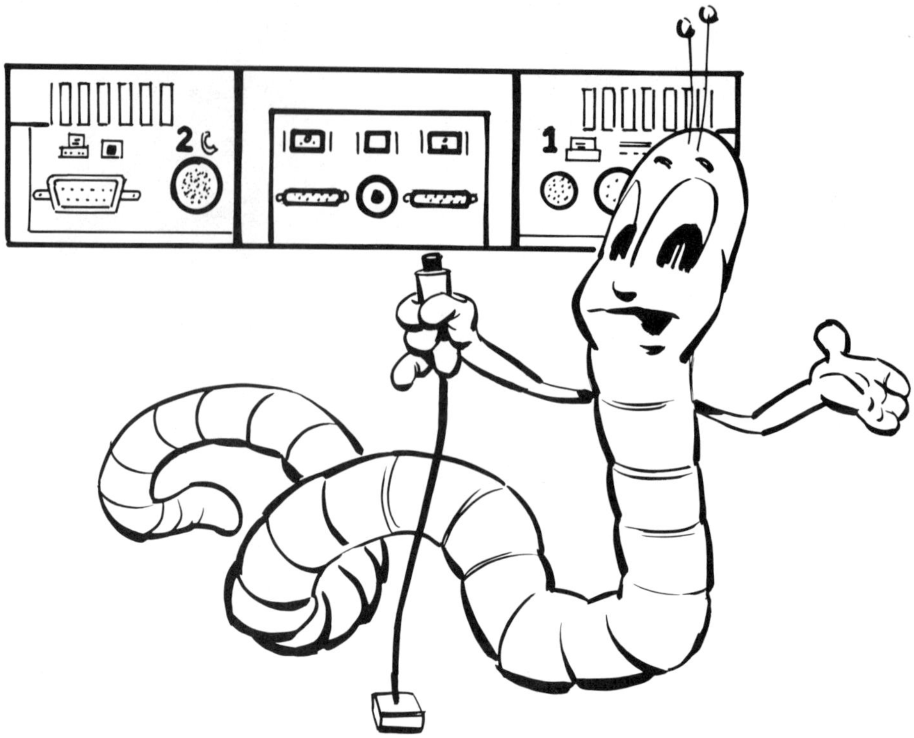

HMMMM! THERE'S NO ICON ON THE PLUG!

The Apple IIc is small but powerful.

The IIc has 128K of RAM memory which is powerful for such a compact, sleek computer. The built-in interface cards which connect the peripherals to the computer through the portals are standard equipment. These have to be purchased separately for other Apple models. The IIc also has a volume control on the left side of the computer, as well as a place to connect earphones. The IIc comes complete with everything a person needs to start using a computer.

Excellent software disks come with the IIc.

Here are the names and descriptions of these disks included with the Apple IIc:

1. Disk one, side one is called "An Introduction." This disk teaches some of the special keys on the keyboard and their uses. Practicing simple exercises at the keyboard helps the user begin to feel at home with the IIc.

2. Disk one, side two is called "The Apple at Play". Several games are on this disk, including the favorite Lemonade and Apple 21. There is even a music recital to illustrate the use of sound and the speaker.
3. Disk two is called "The Apple at Work". This gives examples of the many jobs the IIc can do using software programs, such as word processing. This disk is arranged for both a 40-column and 80-column output. Practice is given for **spreadsheet** entries, software that does math computations and arranges material in tables.

WOW! ALL THIS COMPUTER AND FIVE GREAT DISKS TOO!

Here's more software that comes with the IIc.

4. Disk three, side one is called "The Inside Story". This is a cleverly written computer "detective story" which gives the inside scoop of what goes on under the cover of the IIc. Remember: No one is supposed to remove the cover under threat of forfeiting the warranty. This program was written to satisfy some of the user's curiosity. Explanations are given as to how information is moved around and saved in memory and on disks, etc. inside the computer.

5. Disk three, side two is called "Exploring Apple Logo". First there is a demonstration of **Logo**, which is a popular computer language widely used in grade schools to teach logic and problem solving. Opportunities to write original programs using Logo are offered to the user.
6. Disk four is called "Getting down to BASIC". This is a brief introduction to BASIC to give the user an opportunity to learn how the computer reacts to some simple BASIC commands.

All of these programs are very well written and are an important part of the Apple IIc package.

Three very attractive and colorful manuals also are included with the IIc. The disks and the manuals work together to help a newcomer on a computer feel more at ease.

I ALWAYS ENJOY MY FAVORITE SPREADSHEET.

The System Utilities disk puts the Apple IIc to work.

After getting acquainted with the enjoyable disks mentioned on the preceding pages, the next step is to learn to use an extremely valuable and powerful tool—**the System Utilities disk**, another disk which comes with the Apple IIc. With this disk, you can easily do many different tasks that involve disks, such as copying, initializing, renaming programs, and verifying to see if a disk is useable.

The System Utilities disk is extremely easy to use because all of the instructions are very clear and easy to understand. If you press the [OPEN APPLE] key at the same time you press a question mark, you will receive further directions. You select what you want from the menu when it appears on the screen.

One of the important things you can do with the System Utilities disk is to duplicate your favorite disks. This is called making backups. Just remember: Always cover the write-enable notch or notches of the original disk you are copying with a write-protector tape. This will prevent your copying the wrong disk and erasing what you want to keep.

Make selections from the menu on the screen.

Read the main menu when it appears on the screen to locate the option that reads, "Duplicating a Disk". After you make your selection, a new menu will appear. Now you are to indicate which disk drive you wish to use, either the built-in or the external drive. The disk you want to copy is called the source disk; you must indicate into which drive the source disk is to be placed.

Follow the directions on the screen very carefully and feel free to press the [OPEN APPLE] key and the question mark for additional help if you think you need it. The main thing is to stay relaxed and confident. Take everything one step at a time and follow directions.

Copying is much easier and faster if you have two disk drives. You can leave the original disk in one drive as you copy it on a second disk in the other drive. If you are using just one drive, the source disk must first be copied into memory. Then this disk must be removed and exchanged for the second disk so it can be copied from memory. This, of course, takes more time. Try to get a second disk drive as soon as you can if you don't already have one. It is well worth the money for the added convenience and storage capacity.

The System Utilities disk can format and initialize disks.

The system utilities disk is capable of preparing disks for use with the three operating systems mentioned earlier in the book, DOS 3.3, PASCAL, and ProDOS. There is no longer a need for the DOS 3.3 System Master disk; Apple Computer, Inc., has replaced it with the much more useful System Utilities disk which can do a great deal more with less effort.

Select your choice from the format menu.

Formatting means marking a disk electronically so an operating system can use the disk for reading and writing characters. The menu for formatting on the System Utilities disk is similar to the program for copying. Again, you select your choice from the screen menu.

The Identify and Catalog program lists program information.

This program identifies and catalogs the programs found on a disk. With this catalog, the name of the disk is printed in the upper left hand corner. The type of format of the disk is written in the upper right hand corner, indicating whether the disk is DOS 3.3, ProDOS, or PASCAL. The names of the programs or files are listed in the left-hand column. The center column lists the type of each file, and the column on the right gives the length of each program.

ProDOS has strict rules for writing names of programs.

When using ProDOS, the name of the file or program cannot contain any blank spaces nor any punctuation other than a period. ProDOS names may not be any longer than 15 characters. PASCAL program names may not be longer than seven characters. DOS 3.3 names may be 30 characters long and may contain spaces. It is, however, better to start using names that will be acceptable to ProDOS for all of your programs.

The System Utilities disk has many other functions.

Other uses of the System Utilities disk are to delete or erase a file, rename, lock or unlock a file.

There is an Advanced Operations program which can change the format of a disk and perform other more advanced procedures, such as verifying a disk that has been formatted to make certain it is not damaged in any way.

The ProDOS User's disk is available but not included with the IIc.

This disk is available at extra charge. This program is not as easy for a beginner to understand and use as the System Utilities disk. This software can be used on all the Apple II computers if enough memory is available.

ProDOS is the standard disk operating system of the Apple IIc.

The IIc can use DOS 3.3, PASCAL, and the latest and most powerful operating system, ProDOS. DOS has been used since 1980 and is still used for thousands of programs written for the Apple II computer family. ProDOS can complete some disk operations up to eight times faster than DOS 3.3. Again, this is another example of how new technology has improved computer operating systems.

Some DOS 3.3 commands discussed earlier in the book cannot be used by ProDOS. These commands are FP, INT, and INIT. Check you manual for other details if you want to become a ProDOS expert. There are books and magazines to help you learn more about the specifics of this great system.

If you are just starting out, you should use ProDOS. It is much faster and easier to use than DOS 3.3. Most software manufacturers are designing their programs to be used with ProDOS.

YEAH ProDOS!!

A modem may be attached to the Apple IIc.

A **modem** makes it possible for someone using an Apple IIc, or any other computer, to communicate over long distances. One computer can send messages to another by using a device which can change the digital signals from the computer into analog signals so that messages can be sent over telephone lines. Telephone lines are designed to carry voice-like electronic impulses called analog. Telephone lines cannot transmit digital, or numeric, electronic impulses. The modem is used to make this transition from digital to analog and back again to digital when needed.

LET ME INTRODUCE YOU TO THE APPLE IIc AND ITS MODEM.

From telephone lines, the message can then be sent even greater distances by microwave or satellite transmission. Your computer messages can be sent all over the world if you desire and have connections. Using a computer to communicate over long distances is called **telecommunications**.

YOU CAN BE REPLACED BY A DATA BASE!

At the destination of the message, there must be another modem to change the analog signals coming over the telephone lines back into digital ones so they can be interpreted by the receiving computer.

Special software is needed to use a modem. Most manufacturers of these devices are making software that is useable on the IIc. Make certain the device and software you purchase are compatible with your computer so you can use your IIc to exchange worldwide information.

World-wide information is available to you.

Large assortments of information can be collected into one central source which is called a **data base**. By using telecommunications and your computer, data base information can be brought right into your home. Professional people are using data base services to save thousands of hours of research and reading. If a doctor or lawyer needs certain facts, they use their computers and a data base to quickly sort and find exactly what they need in a matter of seconds! A data base service costs money, but it is well worth the expense if you need information in a hurry. These services should become less expensive as they become more widely used.

Telecommunications is going to change our society in the very near future. Workers will be able to stay home to do much of their work on the computer, then send their work to the office or any destination they desire. This will have a positive effect on the family. It will be beneficial to have fathers and mothers be able to spend more time at home with their children and each other.

Conferences between people scattered over many miles are possible using computers and telecommunications. This will save many trips for tired businessmen.

In the future, students will probably be able to stay home on certain days and send completed lessons done on computers to their teachers when schools incorporate more computer systems for education.

It is an exciting future for all of us. Be flexible enough so you will be able to enjoy it.

Integrated software programs are here at last.

It is now possible to buy one software program that combines three needs into one. These needs are word processing, spreadsheet, and a data base.

Word processing is essential for composing, correcting, and arranging material. Yet sometimes it is necessary to do computations in the middle of a letter or report. This is when a spreadsheet program is necessary. Other times, lists of information need to be added to a letter or report. Then a data base is needed.

THEY REALLY PUT THINGS TOGETHER HERE.

Now all three of these services are rolled into one program called Appleworks. This is one of the most useful software programs ever written. People will probably wonder how they ever managed to work without it.

This software is previewed on one of the disks that comes with the IIc. You will probably want to add it to your disk library as soon as possible.

Which software is usable for which Apple?

Most of the software that has been written is usable for all the Apple II family with few exceptions. You will probably have to extend memory in the Apple II and II Plus because most of the software written is designed for larger RAM memory.

Software is interchangeable between the IIe and IIc. Sometimes a few strange things happen that don't really affect the use of the programs. Check with your Apple dealer if you have problems with a disk that doesn't work on your Apple. He probably can either exchange it or modify it for you so that it will work.

Long lists of programs are available which give the names of software that can be used on particular models. These lists are found in magazines, and your local Apple dealer has information describing the usability of various popular software. This information changes constantly as new software comes on the market, so check before you make a purchase.

The AppleMouse makes graphics a breeze.

You've never seen graphics done as easily as when they are done with AppleMouse. Compared to using the keyboard for drawing, the mouse comes out far ahead in flexibility, fun, and creativity.

The mouse is a small, simple, well-designed yet powerful peripheral. It must be used with software such as MousePaint, which comes with the mouse. MousePaint is an enjoyable way to learn how to use the mouse; it can be used for graphics for home, school, or business.

MousePaint is an adaptation of the remarkable MacPaint software designed for the Apple Macintosh, which is one of the finest software programs ever written. MousePaint is menu driven and uses icons for making selections from the menu. Menu choices along the left side of the screen range from a hand, paint brush, pencil, crayon, spray can, etc. One popular selection is called Fatbits, which can magnify a small section for intricate detail, such as that required for lettering. This program is great fun for people of all ages, especially those that are young in heart!

The first mouse was developed at the Stanford Research Institute in the early 1960s, but the idea was put on the shelf for years until just recently when the usefulness of the mouse was at long last recognized.

Creating and revising complicated graphics are a breeze with the help of "mighty AppleMouse"!

LET MIGHTY APPLEMOUSE DO YOUR GRAPHICS FOR YOU!

The mouse can be used for many other applications.

Other applications for the mouse are springing up like weeds after a rainstorm. Word processing programs featuring the mouse are becoming popular. Several new programs are available and more are on the way. Editing is much simpler using the mouse, since it moves the cursor around the screen with lightning speed and ease. It is still necessary to type rough drafts on the keyboard; then the mouse takes over to edit and make corrections. Spreadsheets are also making effective use of the mouse in moving columns, headings, figures, etc.

The AppleMouse extends some of the flair, drama, and power of the Macintosh to the Apple IIc. With an interface card, software, and adequate memory, the AppleMouse can be used with the IIe and other Apple II computers.

THEY'RE SPRINGING UP LIKE WEEDS AFTER A RAINSTORM!

The future offers many new possibilities as people discover more and more methods to work with this wonderful new tool-the computer. With many new devices being developed to make it ever easier and less threatening to use, the computer will soon be as popular and as necessary as a car.

Apple IIc hardware is unique.

The IIc has hardware that differs from other Apple II family members. For instance, the keyboard has two styles available: the standard keyboard, which is called Qwerty, or the simplified, which is named Dvorak after its designer. (These keyboards are discussed in detail in Chapter 4 if you want more information.) It's always nice to be able to make a choice. Up to this point, computers all came with just one style of keyboard; everyone had to use it whether they thought it was efficient or not. The Apple IIc keyboard also has improved touch and sound sensations which help build speed and accuracy.

IT'S NICE TO HAVE A CHOICE!

There is a also a choice of monitors to use with the IIc. A regular TV set can be used; a TV adaptor is included with the IIc. Because it is so much clearer than a TV, the Apple IIc monitor should be a priority item on your list of equipment to add to your computer. This monitor has a 9-inch green screen and is styled to match the IIc. An attractive matching stand to hold the monitor in various adjustable positions over the computer can also be purchased. These three pieces of equipment—the monitor, stand, and computer—make an attractive package.

A **liquid crystal** display monitor matching the IIc is also available. This small monitor is only about one inch thick and folds flat for storing and portability. It will show 80 columns horizontally and 24 lines vertically. This is the first liquid crystal display that holds more than 16 lines.

IT WORKS LIKE YOUR DIGITAL WATCH,
BUT IT'S A LOT BIGGER.

Where do you go from here? What comes next?

You've made a good start. You know how to write simple programs and know how to use some commercial software. You know where to look for rules in setting up letters, tables, and manuscripts as you use your word processing program.

Be certain to continue. Read other books and magazines. Study programs written by others to see how much you recognize and understand. Attend computer seminars and workshops. Take classes in data processing and programming. Some courses in computer training are offered over television for people who have access to their own computers and printers. Share your knowledge with others. Start teaching your friends and family members who are still a little hesitant about using a computer. Show them that if you can learn to use a computer, they can too.

Keep moving ahead. Be a modern-day pioneer in this computer generation. The rewards are great for those who continue to learn.

SOMETIMES IT'S HARD FOR A WORM TO KNOW WHICH WAY TO TURN.

Which Apple should you buy?

Unless you get an unbelievable deal on one of the older Apple II series to allow for expensive upgrading, it would be wise to purchase either an Apple IIe or IIc. Both the IIe and the IIc are excellent computers; they are designed for different purposes.

The IIc is designed for people who want to start using a computer without having to poke under the computer cover. The IIc is extremely easy to set up; peripherals can be added without having the worry of joining tiny pronged chips. The portals are very simple to use.

The IIc is more economical, even though the original price tag may look higher. The following would have to be added to the Apple IIe to make it as powerful as the IIc: additional memory to bring it up to 128K; a disk drive and interface card; a printer card, an 80-column card; and an interface card for Mouse graphics. With these additions, the price of the IIe exceeds that of the IIc.

The IIe is a better choice for a person who wants to study circuitry and experiment with chips. The IIe can be expanded to have up to four times more memory than the IIc and can be connected to several disk drives at once because of its internal slots. The IIe can also be used with a hard disk which has a huge storage capacity; one hard disk can store all the pages of most books.

Perhaps the best solution would be to buy both machines. Wouldn't it be great to have two Apple computers! This will be very common in many homes in a few years. Families will keep computers very busy.

WHAT SHOULD I DO NOW?

KEEP WORKING ON THAT APPLE!

VOCABULARY TO REMEMBER

Terms

ICON An image or picture used to instruct.

PORTAL Connection or passageway used to interface peripheral equipment.

MODEM A device that links a computer to other computers and information services over telephone lines and other devices.

SPREADSHEET	A type of program that produces a table laid out in columns and rows.
LOGO	A computer language that is easy to learn commonly taught in elementary schools.
SYSTEM UTILITIES DISK	A disk that comes with Apple IIc which gives a person control over the information saved on a disk.
ProDOS	Professional disk operating system. A program that controls the way information is stored on a disk as well as many other tasks.
PASCAL	A computer language that encourages systematic problem solving. Also one of the operating systems available for Apple IIc.
TELECOMMUNICATIONS	Using the computer with communication devices such as modems, telephone lines, satellites, etc.
DATA BASE	A program that keeps track of data. It is used to recall, update, and cross-reference information.
INTEGRATED SOFTWARE	Software program that combines word processing, spreadsheet, and data base into one program. Appleworks is an integrated software program.
LIQUID CRYSTAL MONITOR	Small Apple IIc monitor that folds flat that uses liquid crystal technology.

Creative Corner

Now let's find out what you learned about the Apple IIc and other new things you learned in this chapter.

1. What is different about the Apple IIc?
2. What is a modem?
3. What is telecommunications?
4. Describe an integrated software program.
5. What is MousePaint? How is it unique?
6. What is an icon? Where and why are they used?
7. What is ProDOS?
8. What is Logo?
9. Describe the use of the System Utilities disk.
10. Compare the Apple IIc and IIe. What type of person would prefer the IIc? The IIe?

Congratulations! You've finished the book and have earned your certificate of achievement.

CERTIFICATE OF ACHIEVEMENT

THIS IS TO CERTIFY THAT

____

HAS COMPLETED ALL ASSIGNMENTS FROM
"FIRST NIBBLES OF
THE APPLE COMPUTER"

Melba J. Bennett
Melba J. Bennett

Nibbles
Nibbles

YOU DID IT!

RESERVED WORDS THAT SHOULD NOT BE USED AS VARIABLES

ABS	HTAB	RESTORE
AND	IF	RESUME
ASC	IN#	RETURN
AT	INPUT	RIGHT$
ATN	INT	RND
CALL	INVERSE	ROT=
CHR$	LEFT$	RUN
CLEAR	LEN	SAVE
COLOR=	LET	SCALE=
CONT	LIST	SCRN(
COS	LOAD	SGN
DATA	LOG	SHLOAD
DEF	LOMEN:	SIN
DEL	MID$	SPC(
DIM	NEW	SPEED=
DRAW	NEXT	SQR
END	NORMAL	STEP
EXP	NOT	STOP
FLASH	NOTRACE	STORE
FN	ON	STR$
FOR	ONERR	TAB(
FRE	OR	TAN
GET	PDL	TEXT
GOSUB	PEEK	THEN
GOTO	PLOT	TO
GR	POKE	TRACE
HCOLOR=	POP	USR
HGR	POS	VAL
HGR2	PRINT	VLIN
HIMEN:	PR#	VTAB
HLIN	READ	WAIT
HOME	RECALL	XDRAW
HPLOT	REM	XPLOT

Index